Alfred M. R. GROFF

"I AM"

TETRANTHROPOS,
A CONSCIOUS HUMAN BEING

*INTEGRAL THREEFOLDING
TOWARDS THE FOURTH WAY OF
LOVE*

Bibliografische Information der Deutschen Nationalbibliothek.
Die Deutsche Nationalbibliothek verzeichnet diese Publikation
in der Deutschen Nationalbibliografie; detaillierte bibliografische
Daten sind im Internet über www.dnb.de abrufbar.

© 2020 GROFF, Alfred M.R.
Herstellung und Verlag: BoD – Books on Demand, Norderstedt
ISBN: 9783752643640

a book about consciousness and self-development,
democracy and money,
social and solidarity (associative) economy

**FREEDOM - EQUALITY - HUMANNESS -
SUSTAINABILTY**

MTK a.s.b.l. & ID a.s.b.l. book (editors)

"Tetranthropos"
by Jean-Marie Godar, 2014

TABLE OF CONTENTS

FOREWORD

Alfred Groff gives us practical ways and exercises that help us become more completely who we are, not only as individuals but collectively as whole societies. Today, the global nature of the many problems that confront us highlight the inadequacies of our present culture and its institutions. This demands from us, both deeper levels of introspection, and an outer transformation of our society and economy, locally and globally. In this remarkable book, Groff points the way to both, giving us the personal tools to act inside ourselves and the political tools to act outside in wider society.

JOHN BUNZL

businessman, writer and founder of the
Simultaneous Policy campaign (Simpol)
www.simpol.org

ACKNOWLEDGEMENT

I would like to express my very great appreciation to
John Bunzl (https://simpol.org/who-we-are/who-we-are) and
William Pennell Rock
(https://sacredperformance.com/contact/director-bio/)
for their help with the translation into English.

1. INTRODUCTION

What is the purpose of this book? If you mainly want to REACT all your life and not take responsibility for your own life, then don't read this book.

"Laziness and cowardice are the reasons why such a large part of mankind gladly remain minors all their lives, long after nature has freed them from external guidance. They are the reasons why it is so easy for others to set themselves up as guardians. It is so comfortable to be a minor. If I have a book that thinks for me, a pastor who acts as my conscience, a physician who prescribes my diet, and so on--then I have no need to exert myself. I have no need to think, if only I can pay; others will take care of that disagreeable business for me." (Immanuel Kant, What is Enlightenment?, 30th September, 1784)

But if you are willing to ACT, this book "does not think for you", but it can be an incentive to freely making your own CONSCIOUS choices about your path of development as a HUMAN BEING.

To *react* also means

- to be at the mercy of your "associative" thoughts; to apply "rules" without questioning,
- to be controlled by feelings of sympathy and antipathy; to like your habits too much,
- to sustain longings for sensual stimulations you may regret later; to follow all instincts blindly.

To *act* also means

- to be aware and centred,
- to sense the energy ("reflections of love") in your whole body, here and now : "I AM",
- to be consciously creative and realize your potential.

If you want to realize something in a community, you have to communicate. Two aspects of communication are emphasized here:

- communicating without precise terms ("Begriff" in German) leads to misunderstandings, sometimes with drastic consequences,
- we often use nouns. Nouns are useful to describe things, but much less useful for describing living beings, who are constantly in a state of change and development. Nouns usually lack relativity and don't tell us from what point of view, from what perspective and from what level of consciousness they are used.

What do we mean by

- integral,
- threefolding and fourth way?

INTEGRAL is defined here as seeing a whole from as many perspectives as possible, with a consciousness of maximal depth and width, and from a cosmocentric point of view.
(http://htwins.net/scale/index.html)

To understand a whole it helps to differentiate its main aspects. If we differentiate THREE aspects, we can speak of THREEFOLD-ING. If ONE represents the ABSOLUTE (being, "Sein" in German), THREE represents the triad that stands for the three main forces in the universe, which could be related to:

- "potential" (possibility of doing something, creativity),
- "relationships" (meeting and communicating)
- and "needs (give and take) or to:

- "evolution" ("Werden" in German),
- "consciousness" and
- "actions".

From the point of view of a human being we could differentiate:

- "spirit",
- "soul" and
- "body".

Or, on a psychological level:

- mind,
- feelings and
- will.

In the book we'll play. We will symbolically combine the THREE vertices of a triangle at its centre and we'll get to point number FOUR. The elevated middle of the triangle leads us to a TETRA-HEDRON, the axis of which we'll define as an emanation of the ONE that we will call the "axis of LOVE". We are on the FOURTH WAY!

We will also try to understand many terms and notions used in this book (freedom, will, work, money ...). Only the notion of LOVE can't be understood but only experienced.

> *"It's easy to love a perfect God, unblemished and infallible that He is. What is far more difficult is to love fellow human beings with all their imperfections and defects. Remember, one can only know what one is capable of loving. There is no wisdom without love. Unless we learn to love God's creation, we can never truly love nor truly know God."* (The forty rules of love - Elif Shafak)

In conclusion we could say that this book hopes to assist you in becoming a CONSCIOUS HUMAN BEING, a "TETRAN-THROPOS", who raises the centre of the triangle, representing the triad of life, from its centre as a fourth dimension: "the axis of LOVE". Happiness or even bliss is a consequence and the principal result of hard work. This work is inherent in the will of life, but it is also freely chosen in the multitude of possibilities offered by creation and creativity. You might have to swim against the tide, but in coalition with the will of life you might be able to reach the source!

2. THREEDIMENSIONAL THREEFOLDING

2.1 POINTS and CIRCLE: I and the ABSOLUTE

● ‥‥‥‥‥‥

A point. A point of view! Imagine it is YOUR POINT of view, here and now ... that's how the future begins. Be conscious that this point of view is in a constant state of development, always changing, EVOLVING.

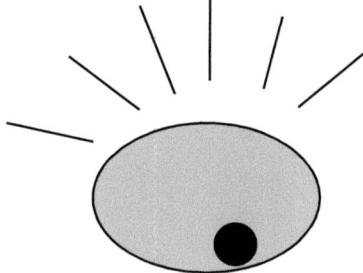

Your POINT of view is one thing, the perspective YOU take is another. Most of the time there are many more perspectives than you are aware of. See in how many directions YOU can look now. Of course, don't forget the headstand perspective! To stand on a mountain or in a valley may change many perceptions.

Depending on the subject at hand, the level of consciousness can also make an enormous difference. And every perspective contains only a partial truth, which is always wrong in an absolute sense.

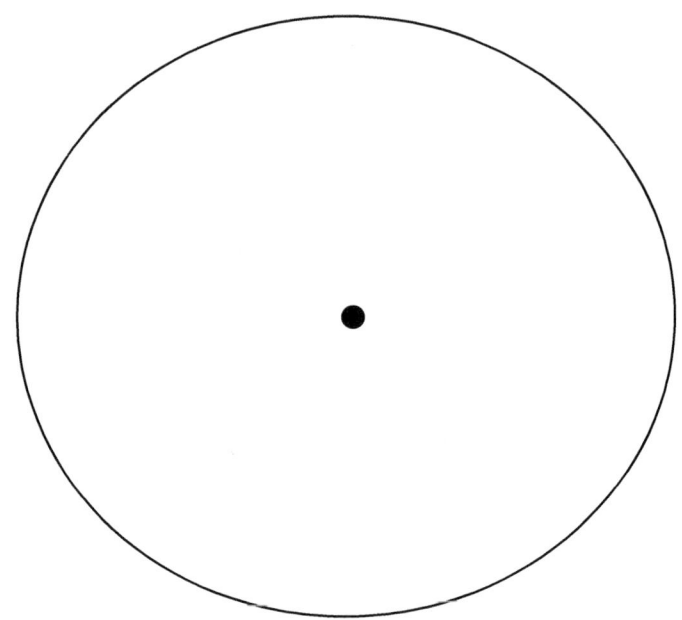

Now imagine a CIRCLE around your POINT of view as a symbol for the ABSOLUTE BEING. YOU are part of it. YOU may feel like this centre, but don't forget that all others may feel likewise, and with just as much right.

Now take a POINT on this circle and call it "My Transpersonal Core" ("Main Transpersonale Kaer – MTK"). Transpersonal, in the sense that it is much greater than YOU as a person. YOU can also call this point YOUR Higher I, or Higher Self or however YOU wish to name it.

Is it right to say that evolution is the "ABSOLUTE" playing with it-self, with each human being a toy in the BEING and BECOMING game?

18

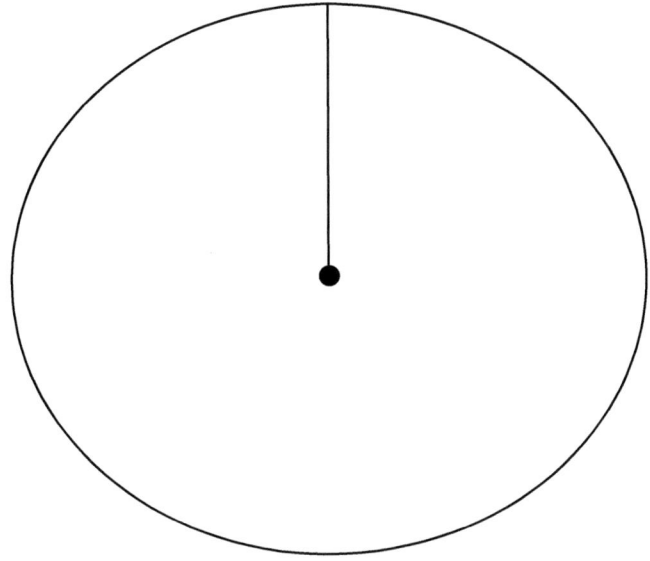

I would like to call "LOVE", "LIFE EROS" or "LIGHT" the ray that connects the middle of the circle with YOUR transpersonal core on the circle itself. How does it feel to be touched in this way? ... to let live. The future of life is calling YOU! YOU are free how to respond.

Even if we have to find answers to our life to achieve our aims, we can never force life. We can only meet life. We can feel what life wants from us personally and decide how to be active. Everybody needs life and life needs everybody: „active involvement and receptive receiving", giving and taking.

●   ●

Two POINTS - Polarity: now there's an opposite. We can meet.
This is very useful for our consciousness (the potential relationship
between the two points is the third hidden element in this setup).

A third POINT creates a dynamic moment. Something new develops. A triad. Triads will accompany us through the whole book.

Let's name the three points with colours: yellow, blue and red.

Associations with yellow: rationality, clear thinking, openness, light, the sun...
Associations with blue: harmony, friendship, air, water, longing, trust...
Associations with red: energy, strength, desire, powerful health...

We will see...

●

●

●   ●

Imagine a fourth POINT in the middle of the three others: Tetra!
(Greek: four)

Possible evolution?

2.2 TETRAHEDRONS and COLOURS:

the INDIVIDUAL and the SOCIAL ORGANISM

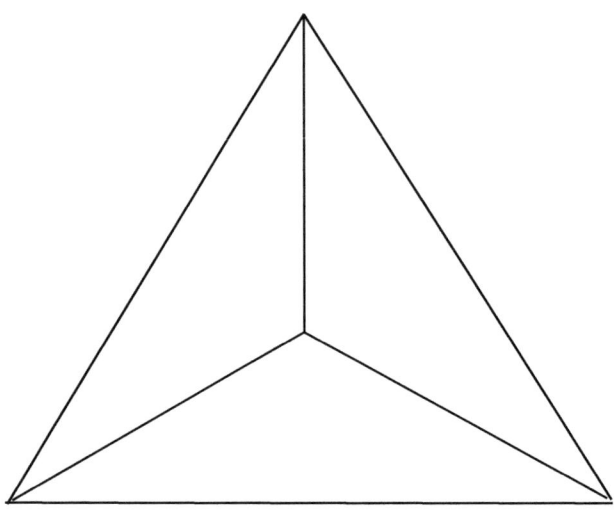

Let's connect all four points and imagine the middle rises in the third dimension, so that all the corners (4 points) are an equal distance from each other. This is an equilateral tetrahedron seen from above.

According to Wikipedia *a tetrahedron is a polyhedron composed of four triangular faces, three of which meet at each vertex. It has six edges and four vertices. The tetrahedron is one kind of pyramid, which is a polyhedron with a flat polygon base and triangular faces connecting the base to a common point. In the case of a tetrahedron the base is a triangle (any of the four faces can be considered the base). A tetrahedron is also known as a "triangular pyramid".* The upper vertex can have different meanings and can represent different topics, as we'll see. The three external points of the base can be seen as aspects of the upper vertex of the tetrahedron. These aspects stand for different realms and have different qualities. We can speak of threefolding as looking at three realms of a topic; three distinct autonomous aspects of an integral organism.

a tetrahedron

Now let's attribute different colours to the aspects at hand. In the picture you can see a red tetrahedron. But what does it mean if I write: In every "red" tetrahedron there are also "yellow" and „blue aspects"? The colours stand for different qualities of each aspect.

Let's take a school as an example. The aim of a school is to provide information and to develop skills. A school is neither a bank nor a parliament. And yet there are, nevertheless, monetary incomes and expenditures like in a bank, as well as special rules, similar to the laws decided in a parliament.

If we talk about living organisms, the complexity becomes even greater, especially if we talk about human beings, like in this book.

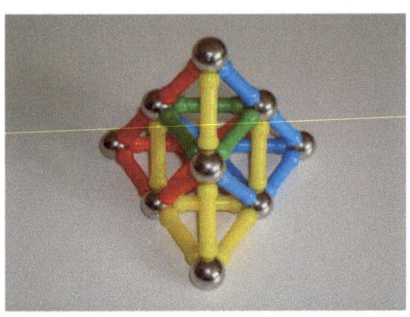

the individual organism:
body and consciousness

In this picture we see an INDIVIDUAL ORGANISM and its inner life, shown as a 4-coloured tetrahedron.

As with every tetrahedron, this one can be divided into its four corner-tetrahedrons:

One with a yellow base, one with a blue base, and one with a red base. And on top, one with a green base.

In all four tetrahedrons we find yellow, blue and red aspects.

- The tetrahedron with the green base shows the material body of a person. This body is part of nature. This means that the upper vertex stands for the physical body.

the human being: inner aspects

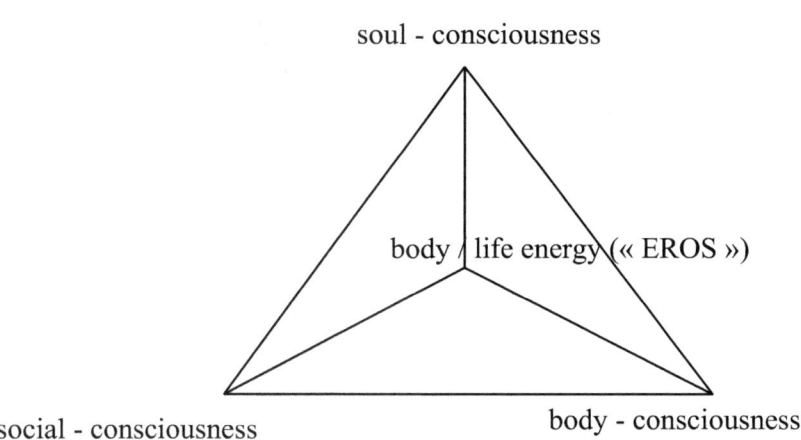

In this living body we can find the internal parts of a person, of which the person is more or less aware. A human being has the potential for integral consciousness.

We can name these parts:

- soul-consciousness (tetrahedron with the yellow base)
- social-consciousness (tetrahedron with the blue base)
- body-consciousness (tetrahedron with the red base)

the social organism:
nature and culture

Let's go further and imagine the same tetrahedron once again.
But now we change the perspective and look outwardly.

This time the tetrahedron stands for the outside world of a person,
the SOCIAL ORGANISM (nature and society).

- The tetrahedron with the green base stands for nature.

the human being: outside view

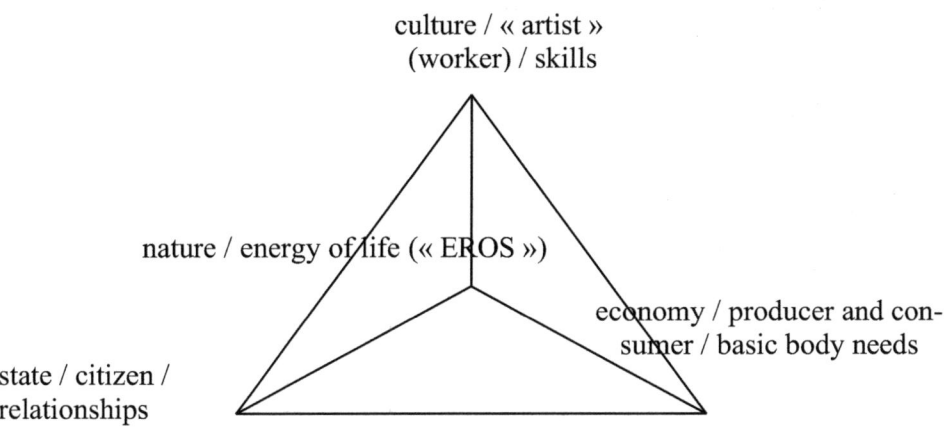

culture / « artist »
(worker) / skills

nature / energy of life (« EROS »)

economy / producer and consumer / basic body needs

state / citizen /
relationships

- Culture in general is based on nature.

- We divide this general culture into

- culture in the narrowest sense (tetrahedron with the yellow base)
- the state (tetrahedron with the blue base)
- economy (tetrahedron with the red base).

Every human being is constantly involved in these three areas: as a member of civil society, as a citizen, or as a producer/consumer.

"three dimensional map of the human being"

If we put two tetrahedrons on top of each other, with their upper vertexes touching each other, we have a special double tetrahedron. It represents the inner and outer realities of a human being. The middle point, which represents the human body, is part of nature and symbolises your point of view, your experience and your behavior - here and now.

The head, the sphere on top, represents the integral witness with its multiple perspectives: The "Witness – I". Here you can find human consciousness, which can attest to its inner and outer development.

the individual organism, the social organism and the "witness - I"

2.3 THREE TETRAHEDRONS:

FREEDOM, EQUALITY and HUMANNESS

"I am" and the three tetrahedrons:

the individual organism, the social organism and the "transpersonal"

Imagine, a third tetrahedron above the head, which represents the „transpersonal tetrahedron" (going beyond the personal aspects of a human being). The upper vertex of this tetrahedron represents "My Transpersonal Core", "my Highest Self", the "I AM" (the point on the circle representing "the Absolute"). The three aspects or manifestations of this tetrahedron are:

- will of life (the associated colour is yellow)
- diversity (the associated colour is blue)
- creativity (the associated colour is red)

The personal, the social and the transpersonal tetrahedrons represent the three-dimensional version of the "map" of a human being.

34

„TRANSPERSONAL WISDOM"
("LOVE")

| Creativity (word / name / ideas) „humaness" | diversity (richness / kingdom) „equality" | will of life ("Will") „liberty" |

„MAP" OF THE HUMAN BEING

integral
WITNESS-
SELF
with multiple
perspectives

INTEGRAL THREEFOLDING

fear: senselessness / danger: escape	fear: loneliness / danger: fight	fear: death-illness / danger: adherence
consciousness of my skills (self-realization / sense)	consciousness of inner & external relationships (integration / recognition)	consciousness of my physical needs (food / protection)

| thinking | feeling | wanting / judgments | context and theme | empathy | being moved / meanings | sensory perception | breathing | Actions / movements |

| **SOUL-SELF** I can | **SOCIAL-SELF** I meet | **BODY-SELF** I need |

ethereal flow of life

the individual organism

| system of nerves and senses | rhythmical breath and blood circulations | methabolic system and limbs |

EXPERIENCING & ACTING HERE AND NOW

| natural processes (evolution) | regeneration of nature (balance) | natural resources (gifts) |

the social organism

cosmic flow of light - energy - information

| **"ARTIST"** I liberate | **CITIZEN** I communicate | **"LABOURER"** I donate |

| the "true" (science) | the "beautiful" (art) | the "good" (core values) | ideas and initiatives | discussions | decisions | production (give) | trade | consumption (take) |

| collective spiritual flow of knowledge and information (CULTURE) | political and legal development processes and the flow of money (STATE) | flow of services and goods (ECONOMY) |

| BASE OF FREEDOM: holistic information / education | BASE OF EQUALITY: direct and representative democracy | BASE OF SOLIDARITY: guaranteed basic income (+micro finance +regional money) |

TETRANTHROPOS
the conscious human being in a process of evolution

Two-dimensional map of a human being

In the illustrated "human map" (or "map" of the human being) the POINT in the middle of the circle of Chapter 2 ("experiencing and acting here and now") is located at the height of the navel. This place is the intersection of the BODY, which accommodates the INNER LIFE as a guest, NATURE, (green is the colour associated with body and nature), and the CULTURE we are all part of. Take time to meditate on all the aspects and perspectives of the human being. They are all continuously present, even if you are not always aware of it.

The two-dimensional map of the human being looks like a person sitting in the Lotus position wearing a hat.

	LIBERTY
	EQUALITY
	HUMANNESS

Let's take another look at the map of the human being and reflect on the colours which symbolise the quality of every aspect of the human being (3 dimensions):

- yellow stands for the quality or ideal of LIBERTY,
- blue for EQUALITY (equal rights / cosmocentric empathy) and
- red for HUMANNESS (solidarity).

Note that the order of the colours is inverted if we compare the individual and the social with the transpersonal aspects of the human being (meditation in the next chapter).

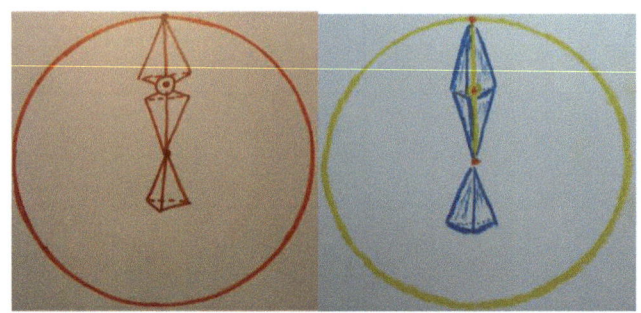

The shining of love („LOVE" / „LIFE-EROS") penetrates the three tetrahedrons passing through their vertices and centres and represents their „backbone".

"I feel another force, not a power that I possess but one in which I am. ... It is this energy, a cosmic force passing in us, that all traditions call "love"."
(Jeanne de Salzmann, The reality of being, p.267)

the HUMAN BEING: here and now

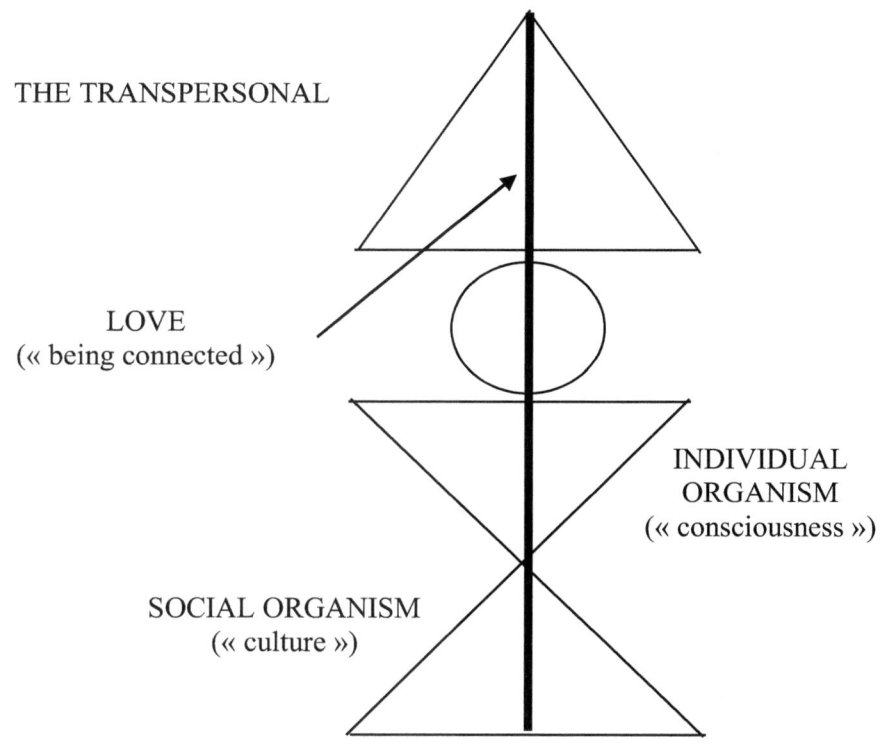

THE TRANSPERSONAL

LOVE
(« being connected »)

INDIVIDUAL
ORGANISM
(« consciousness »)

SOCIAL ORGANISM
(« culture »)

LOVE connects us with all and everything.

"I cannot love outside consciousness. Love is a quality of consciousness. If I wish to know what is, I have to realize that neither words nor the feelings that accompany them are perceptions of reality. The word is not the fact, the feeling is not the fact. They are both the reaction of my conditioning to impressions, to everything that impresses me."
(Jeanne de Salzmann, The reality of being, p.69)

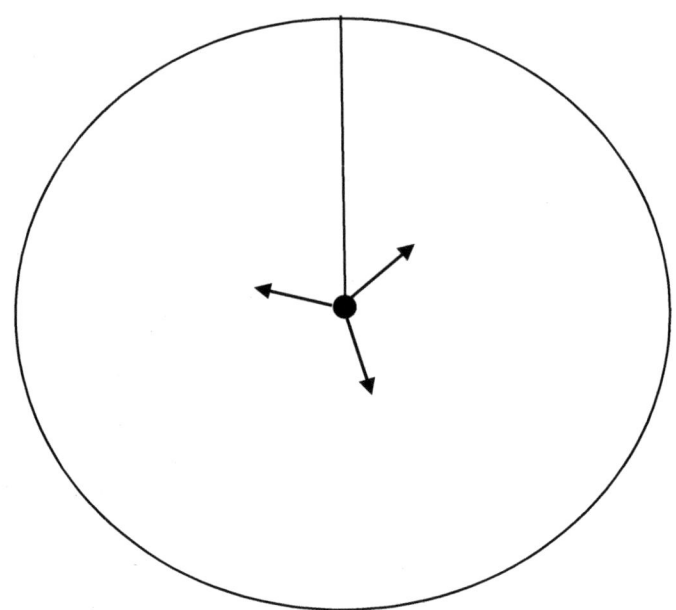

In the beginning there was the POINT representing the ABSO-LUTE. One day, by the action of the WILL OF LIFE, this point expanded in every direction. A SPHERE was born (with the circle as its two-dimensional representation). This sphere still represents the ABSOLUTE. From here emanates the higher "I" of every human being with all its potentials. These potentials are limited through forms (the personal and the social tetrahedrons as well as the body). We call the inside of the sphere the DIVERSITY of reality. In the middle of the circle we find a point which now represents every single being on earth. CREATIVITY means human beings have been created to live a life on earth and they have a creative potential. Their aim is to put this potential into practice for the well-being of the whole. Therefore they have to transcend the forms, develop the consciousness of their witness-self, and be connected with the stream of LOVE:

"I AM" online, "I AM IN LOVE"

3. TRANSPERSONAL WISDOM: CONSCIOUSNESS

Now we have designed a transpersonal map of the human being (two- and three-dimensional). This should have been fairly easy to follow, at least for those of you who are mind-centred. But as mentioned in the introduction it's you who have to *act*, to work. The easy part is now over! In chapter 3 you will need to meditate (with your thoughts, feelings, will, intuition ...). In chapter 4 you will need to change the routines in your daily life (remember permanently what YOU want).

The text and pictures in this book can be an incentive, but you have to do the work! And that's not so easy. It needs a lot of motivation, will-power and power of endurance. There are millions of reasons not to do it now. But if you want to improve your life, you need to make changes, to develop your being, to create a new world. What do you have to lose?

The following two chapters present some material, but it's as if the book is not written yet: you have to write it for yourself. Enjoy!

The main income from work is not money, but more sense and satisfaction in your life, as well as improved conscious relationships. If this is not the case, think of changing the way you work.

3.1 YELLOW MEDITATION

"TRANSPERSONAL MEDITATION"

	„TRANSPERSONAL WISDOM" („LOVE")	
CREATIVITY **(word, name, ideas)** **"HUMANNESS"**	**DIVERSITY** **(richness, kingdom)** **"EQUALITY"**	**WILL OF LIFE** **("Will")** **"LIBERTY"**

- Meditate on the words.
- Meditate on the order of the colours.
- Meditate on the orange "double-octahedron", the "witness I" (see next two pages).

Have a careful look at two of the three tetrahedrons and their colours.

In the picture you see the transpersonal tetrahedron on top of the personal inner tetrahedron (the head that we imagined in between both is not visible and the body-part of the personal tetrahedron is cut off, so you only see the green base of the body tetrahedron).

If you take a tetrahedron and look at the four small corner tetrahedrons, the space between the four tetrahedrons is an octahedron (in orange, inside the transpersonal tetrahedron on the picture). We can imagine that this orange double octahedron (one inside the personal and one inside the transpersonal tetrahedrons) is the "head", which we earlier represented as a yellow circle/globe (page 58 in the map) – it is the connection between the personal and transpersonal worlds and helps to make this relationship a conscious one (note that orange is the complementary colour of blue - consciousness of inner and outer relationships in the map of the human being).

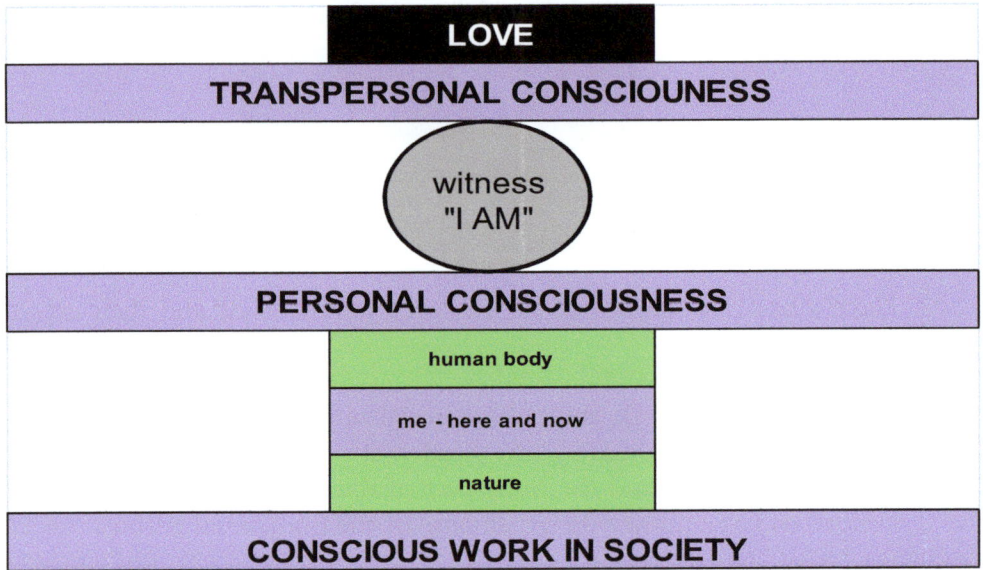

3.2 YELLOW MEDITATION

"TETRANTHROPOS MAP -
STREAM OF LIFE MEDITATION"

1

4	3	2
	5	
6	7	8
	9	
10	11	12

- 1 represents the Absolute
- 4 3 2 represent the transpersonal level
- 5 represents the witness
- 6 7 8 represent the inner-personal level (soul-, relationship- and body-consciousness)
- 9 represents nature and our body, being part of nature
- 10 11 12 represent acting in the different domains of society (outer-social)

- 1
  4 3 2 represent the upper tetrahedron (transpersonal)

- 5 (witness)
  6 7 8 or 6 7 8
                 9 (body) represent the middle tetrahedron (personal)

  9 (nature)
10 11 12 represent the lower tetrahedron
                     (society, culture in a broad sense)

Is this a logical sequence representing the stream of life from the Absolute towards our physical body in 9 stages, the last stage being love returning to its source, the Absolute?

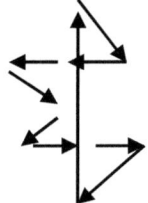

The Absolute is the source of the triad "will of life – diversity – creativity" (transpersonal level). Through the will of life I am confronted with the diversity of everything that exists (possibilities of life). Creativity (possibility of creation through my I) helps me to incarnate on earth. The Witness-I connects the transpersonal level with the personal one. On the personal level we find the Soul-I (consciousness of my potential), the social-I (consciousness of my inner and outer relationships) and the Body-I (consciousness of my physical needs). My personal consciousness makes me responsible for the actions of my body in the here and now, in the nature of the planet earth and in different domains of society. Everything done in the spirit of real love returns to the source and becomes immortal.

"What is an octave?
You may remember that do, re, mi, fa, sol, la, si, do form an octave, but that it is unknown what these sounds represent. Perhaps you also know that intervals occur in the octave, namely between re-mi and si-do. Chapter 7 of In Search of the Miraculous discusses this subject thoroughly.

The names of the octave can be derived from (see A. Blake):

DO   - DOminus
SI   - SIdera
LA   - via LActea
SOL - SOL
FA   - FAta
MI   - MIcrocosmos
RE   - REgina coelum
DO   - DOminus

So here you can see the names appear of what Gurdjieff and Ouspensky called the Ray of Creation:

Do   - the Absolute
Si   - all Galaxies
La   - this Milky Way
Sol   - Sun
Fa   - Planets
Mi   - Earth
Re   - Moon
Do   - the Absolute."

(Dorine van Oyen, The Octave and the 'Primavera',
http://gurdjieffclub.com)

You can also meditate, if you find any connections with
- the 12 (3x4) of astrology,
- the 9 of the Enneagram (1, 3, 6 and 7),
- the 7 notes. The half tones between MI and FA and SI and DO could they represent the descent from the transpersonal to the personal level and from the personal level to the body?

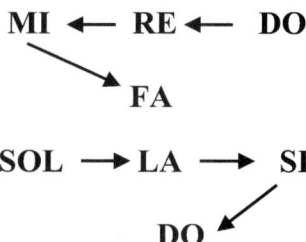

or the ascent from the personal level to the transpersonal level and from there to the Absolute?

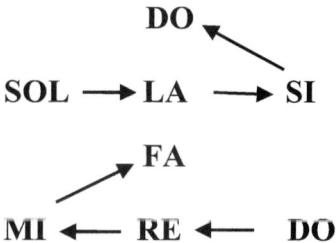

If you think of half tones, can you draw a tetrahedron with one line without lifting the pen from the paper?

3.3 YELLOW MEDITATION

"TETRANTHROPOS MAP - COLOUR MEDITATION"

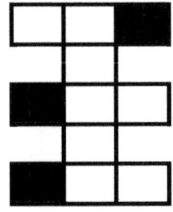

YELLOW (LIBERTY)

Transpersonal: Will of life, Will (spiritual).
Personal: soul-self, consciousness of own skills,
self-realization, meaning of life, thinking.
Social: being an artist or a scientist in the search for the truth,
liberation of own skills.

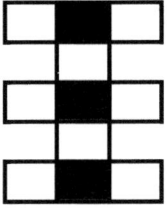

BLUE (EQUALITY / EQUAL RIGHTS)

Transpersonal: diversity of existence, richness of creation,
"kingdom".
Personal: social-self, consciousness of internal and external
relationships, integration, empathy and recognition.
Social: being a citizen in communication, right to participate and
decide in society.

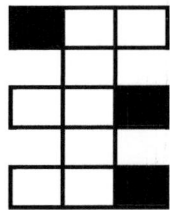

RED (HUMANNESS / SOLIDARITY)

Transpersonal: creation and creativity, ideas and terms.
Personal: body-self, consciousness of physical needs,
movements.
Social: taking as a consumer and being a worker, a producer of
goods and services.

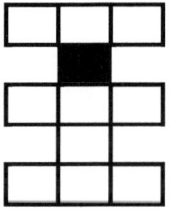

ORANGE

The witness: the bridge between red (transpersonal creativity) and
yellow (personal potential).

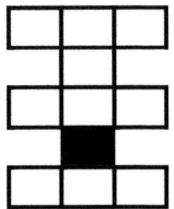

GREEN

<u>Nature and bodies</u>: bearers of souls (yellow) in social interaction (blue).

"The sensory world is the school, without which the human being would never come to the spirit"
(Rudolf Steiner - Leipzig, June 30th, 1906)

You also can meditate sub-colours like blue in yellow (for example feelings in the soul: equal rights in the field of freedom) or red in blue (for example decisions in democratic processes: humanness in the field of equal rights).

3.4 YELLOW MEDITATION

"TETRANTHROPOS - the CONSCIOUS HUMAN BEING - and the SEVENFOLD WORK"

I am in the "Absolute", I am in the world.

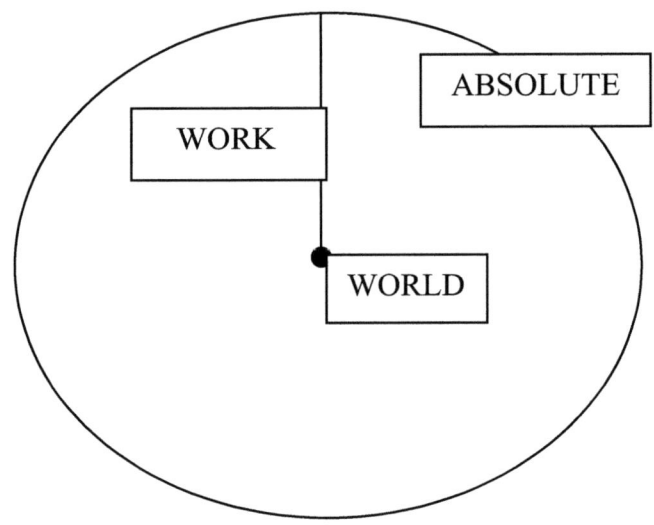

I have to work and let it work.

I am the work.

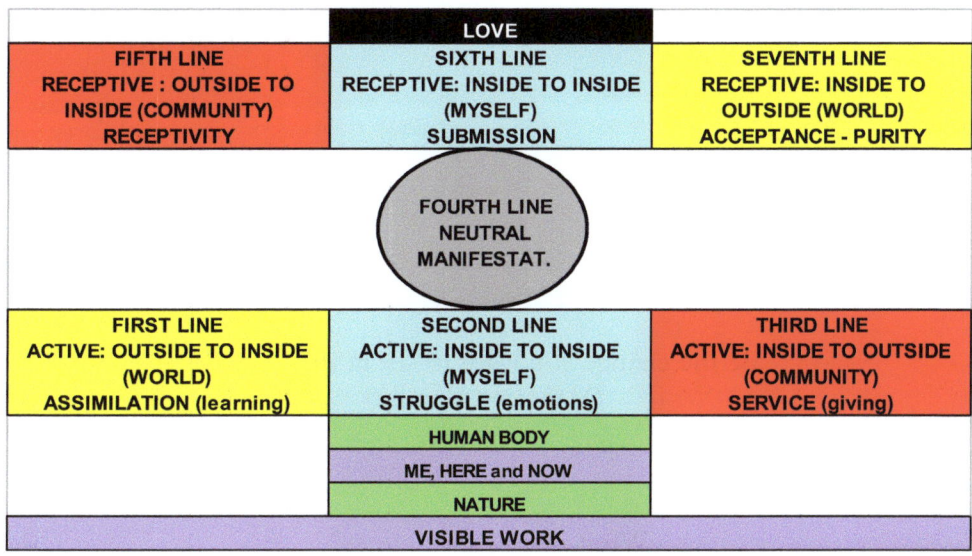

	LOVE	
FIFTH LINE **RECEPTIVE : OUTSIDE TO** **INSIDE (COMMUNITY)** **RECEPTIVITY**	**SIXTH LINE** **RECEPTIVE: INSIDE TO INSIDE** **(MYSELF)** **SUBMISSION**	**SEVENTH LINE** **RECEPTIVE: INSIDE TO** **OUTSIDE (WORLD)** **ACCEPTANCE - PURITY**
	FOURTH LINE **NEUTRAL** **MANIFESTAT.**	
FIRST LINE **ACTIVE: OUTSIDE TO INSIDE** **(WORLD)** **ASSIMILATION (learning)**	**SECOND LINE** **ACTIVE: INSIDE TO INSIDE** **(MYSELF)** **STRUGGLE (emotions)**	**THIRD LINE** **ACTIVE: INSIDE TO OUTSIDE** **(COMMUNITY)** **SERVICE (giving)**
	HUMAN BODY	
	ME, HERE and NOW	
	NATURE	
	VISIBLE WORK	

"the seven LINES
of the sevenfold WORK*"

	WORLD **(active learning and will of life)**
	MYSELF **(emotions and diversity)**
	COMMUNITY **(giving and creativity)**

* J.G. Bennett: The sevenfold Work, Claymont (1979)

"Be the change you want to see in the world"
(Mahatma Gandhi)

What is consciousness?

1. What do I do? (knowledge, „witness")

2. Why do I do it? (for whom?)

3. Do „I my-SELF" want to do it?
   (my transpersonal core)

3.5 BLUE MEDITATION

"CARRIAGE-MEDITATION and FEELINGS"

Imagine a horse-drawn carriage with a driver and a passenger.*

- The carriage represents the human body.
- The driver represents the human mind.
- The horse represents the human will.
- The passenger represents the Higher I.

But what represents the human emotions and feelings?

Feelings facilitate relations. Relations produce feelings.
Feelings are like a barometer between concerned entities, the in-between. Without them the carriage couldn't work properly. They allow for necessary dialogue and communication. They indicate the quality of a relationship. Take them in account, but don't identify with them or stick with them for too long. What ties occur in our imagined carriage? These ties represent our feelings and emotions.

- The voice: between the driver (mind) and the passenger (Higher I / WILL of life, "I AM")
- The harness and the reins: between the driver (mind) and the horse (will)
- The seat: between the driver (mind) and the carriage (body)
- The shaft: between the carriage (body) and the horse (will)

What comes to your mind, your feelings and your body if you meditate on the above image? The ride and its quality represent the doing (work) and the road represents nature in which we live. What if you have a relationship consisting of two people? Two horses will draw the two connected carriages, two drivers can switch their position, but where will the passengers sit: Together in one carriage or each one in his/her own? And the feelings …? This leads us to the next meditation!

* Georg I. Gurdjieff writes about another perspective of a horse-drawn carriage.

3.6 BLUE MEDITATION

"HIGHER I and ORDINARY I IN RELATIONSHIPS"

MEDITATION about the interplay of the HIGHER I and LOVE with the ORDINARY I of everyday life in a personal RELATION-SHIP-TRIAD

PART 1: FOOD FOR THOUGHTS

A personal relationship-triad consists of three different dimensions that can appear in personal relationships separately or in common, in very different versions.

LOVERS, who share INTIMACY (I AM+I AM)

- Energetic nearness and a common energy field experience (also possibly on physical distance).
- Meditate, share and experience energetic-spiritual streams and the ray of love.
- Feel body contact (touch, caress, hold, sensuous contact, kiss) and investigate tantric-meditative sexuality together.
- Live the ray of love in a common exchange as a service to the higher I.

FRIENDS, who share INTERESTS (WE)

- Feel secure in being together and/or in mutual exchange (connection with sympathy).
- Promote their common development through communication, including solving conflicts/disputes.
- Have interesting discussions about common interest fields.
- Plan, execute and look retrospectively at stimulating common projects/undertakings.

PARTNERS, who share SUPPLY (maintenance of the basis of life) (IT)

- Common household (or an apartment-sharing community).
- Common parenthood (or care of relatives in need).
- Common everyday life arrangements; importance of showing off social status.
- Economic-financial security for the fulfilment of basic needs.

Some relations may primarily be love relationships, amicable or co-operative relations, other rather hybrid types of relationship like loving friendships or amicable partnerships. Many people are dreaming of the ideal partner, of soul complementarity, or simply of the "prince" or "princess", who improves one's own life, saves us or fulfils our every wish and does so „until death us do part". Some questions:

- If I have found the ideal partner, how long do I think this state will last?
  And if it lasts longer, would I really lack nothing, like excitement, curiosity, or the opportunity for further self-development...?
- If I do not find the ideal relationship, would I prefer to have no relationship at all?
- Do I accept discomfort only to get some of my needs met, or because of fears I may have?
- Do I expect too much from my partner? Am I prepared to compromise?
- Am I succumbing to illusions or to possessive claims?
- Do I accept or even suffer from our common sexuality? Is there even some exploitation?

- Do I accept development, fluctuation and changes in the relationship? Do I change my relationships too fast or too slowly?
- How open can I be? Do I exclude some subjects from our dialogue?
- Do I perceive my projections? Am I disturbed by aspects of my partner, which I recognise in myself and which I don't like at all?

Am I conscious of both the inner and outer dimensions of an intimate relationship, an interest community, or a care community? Before I jump to saying that these are „many words, many thoughts, many questions" or that this is "too much theory", I should at least be aware of how much "Ego" I am prepared to let go of. How much "Ego" would I like to preserve in my everyday life and how will I handle the clash of our two "Egos"?

PART 2: COMMUNICATION

Which of the above points are really important to me or to my partner? How often do I, or does he/she, want this or that? How big are the differences between us? How can we openly and honestly discuss it? Did we discuss/find a suitable compromise for our practical every day life? Or do we hope that life will fix it if we only "love one another"?

Finally, after analysing my thoughts and my communications, let's return to myself.

- What do I feel inwardly? What do I feel empathically when I concentrate on my partner?
- What does the Higher I want for my relationship?
- What do I miss?
- What do I and the Higher I call love? Am I ready to love myself?
- Am I ready to make gifts?

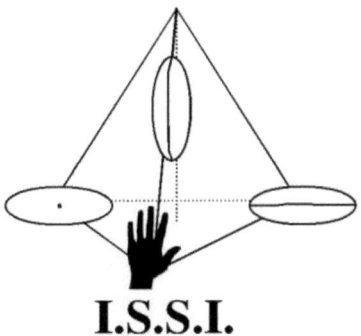

I.S.S.I.

individual - sensual – sexual (EROS) – intimate

"Love starts when we push aside our ego and make room for someone else."
(Rudolf Steiner)

3.7 BLUE MEDITATION

"DODECAHEDRON and THE 12"

We already met the tetrahedron with its four triangular faces. We talked about three tetrahedrons (personal, transpersonal, social) with 12 triangular faces. After encountering the octahedron as well, we are coming to the regular dodecahedron, composed of twelve regular pentagonal faces.

3 tetrahedrons = 12 faces - 1 dodecahedron = 12 faces

Plato said: *"It is impossible for two things to cohere without the intervention of a third."*
So, if we classify the platonic solids in a triad "male" - "relation m/f (child)" - "female", a tetrahedron would be "male", an octahedron would be "relation" (we spoke of "connection between the personal and transpersonal worlds" before), and a dodecahedron would be "female".

We could say that the tetrahedral map with all the components and sub-components of the three tetrahedrons involved is a rather logical ("male") way to look at the human being.

You can unfold a dodecahedron to arrive at the symbol of a human being with one face as the middle part (heart and stomach). On the 4 edges you find attached 2 pentagonal faces (2 legs and 2 arms) and on one edge three faces (neck, head and "Witness self").

One reason why a dodecahedron is "female" concerns its pentagonal faces, the number five. In the ancient world a pentagram was the symbol of Venus, the planet of the Goddess. Pythagoras was especially interested in the mathematical aspect of the golden ratio. Five inferior conjunctions of the planet Venus repeat in a recessing pentagram. In the Bible, the female (Eve) is related to the apple with its five seeds.

Here we associate the dodecahedron with the 12 senses of a human being:

The "physical" senses (lower senses)

1. touch (in German: "Tastsinn")
2. life ("Lebenssinn"), allows the activities of the inner organs to be perceived (pain, fatigue...)
3. movement ("Eigenbewegungssinn"), allows proprioception
4. balance ("Gleichgewichtssinn"), allows vestibular perceptions

The "feeling" senses (middle senses)

5. smell
6. taste
7. sight
8. warmth

The "awareness" senses (upper senses)

9. hearing ("Hörsinn" / "Lautsinn")
10. speech ("Sprachsinn" / "Wortsinn")
11. awareness of another's thoughts ("Gedankensinn")
12. I ("Ichsinn"), total empathy for the essence of the other person

In a dodecahedron, lying on a table, the lower face could symbolize touch and the upper face the sense of "I". An empathetic feeling of your "I AM", is also being conscious of my and our "I AM".

NOW WE PROPOSE A DANCE-MEDITATION WHICH FA-
CILITATES "FEELING LIFE THROUGH ALL YOUR
SENSES".

Experience the twelve aspects of the human being in motion
through your twelve senses in a "dodecahedral dance", which you
can perform alone, as a couple, or in a group.

A predefined choreography is unnecessary. Be inspired in the here
and now and *feel*, don't think, don't be logical. Try instead to be integral in the sense of experiencing a whole with as many perspectives
as possible, with a consciousness of maximal depth and width and
from a cosmo-centric point of view. Don't identify with your experiences. Enjoy!

I AM

What HE THINKS HE can create
(goal in the future)

What SHE FEELS in diversity
(here and now)

What WE DONATE consciously and lovingly to life
(realize our potential from the past through actions here and now
for the common future)

Link: Ken Wilber and I AMness (put these words in google or go to

http://www.youtube.com/watch?v=BA8tDzK_kPI)

3.8 RED MEDITATION

"www-meditation : will, want, work"

Needs and fears

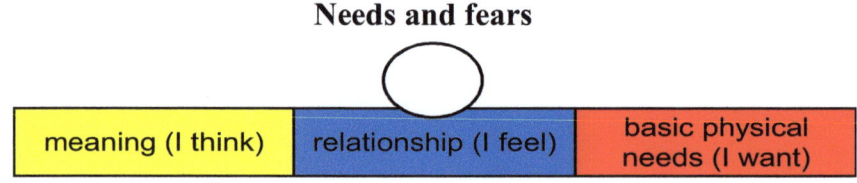

meaning (I think)	relationship (I feel)	basic physical needs (I want)

individual needs

fear of senselessness	fear of solitude	fear of death / illness

- **What is "WANT"?**

What I normally want, concerns my everyday needs - it is mostly an egoistic point of view. Do I know what my needs are? Especially my physical needs can be met by the economy.

There are three main categories of needs, which are connected to my three primal fears:

- the physical needs of food, drink, warmth, security and the fear of illness, death,
- the social needs of relationship, recognition and the fear of solitude,
- the higher needs of self-development, meaning of life and the fear of senselessness.

Meditation:

If I can eat and drink what I really like, if my sexual needs were met, if I have no financial problems, a good relationship with my partner and my family, as well as many friends, if I read interesting books and have good discussions, enjoy a satisfying leisure time with fun activities and travelling if I'd like to .... Does this mean that all my needs met? Do I miss anything? What could that be?

CONSCIOUSNESS: multiperspective, integral recognition of the individual POTENTIAL	POSITIVISM: Seeing how to put things into practice through the ENCOUNTER with the multitude of possibilities in the outside world	ACTION: DOING it and overcoming automatic customary functioning, laziness, passivity, sleepy states

```
┌──────────────────────┐
│         „I"          │
│   Individuality /    │
│     Human being      │
└──────────────────────┘

┌──────────────────────┐
│  Regular practice /  │
│ "WORK"/development   │
└──────────────────────┘
```

- **What is "WILL"?**

There are different levels of will: first there is the transpersonal "Will of life", there is the will as part of the personal soul, there is the will of the body including unconscious instincts and there is the will expressed in a deed. The will can be motivated by the highest ranging to the lowest motivations for satisfaction of purely egoistic needs. Do I know my potentials? Do I develop my skills? Do I realize my potentials? Do I fulfil the purpose of my life in expressing the "Higher Will", in donating my deeds to other beings ...?

Playing stupid, identifying with "learned" aspects of knowledge instead of being creative ("I can't do that ")	Criticizing negatively ("he/she/it does/doesn't do /is/is not")	Being reactive and falling into depressive states ("it doesn't work ")

ACTIVE (HUMAN BEING)	REACTIVE (PC=Programmed Computer)
Suffering = Overcoming laziness through conscious effort	
Following my artistic imagination FREELY and CREATIVELY	Thinking and talking associatively (knowing instead of understanding) – Importance of money, consumption, appearance
Meeting diversity with a LOVING attitude and being conscious that I do to myself what I do to the whole	Being driven by judgmental prejudices and feelings of sympathy and antipathy - importance of power
Acting with respect, i.e. acting on the basis of my POTENTIAL (for myself and for others)	Following instinctively the sensations of lust – importance of addictive cravings for food, drinks, drugs, sex...

<u>Meditation</u>:

Tetranthropos is a conscious human being. What am I conscious of?

- What do I do? Is the "Witness-I" involved and what
does he observe?
- Why do I do it? For whom? What is my motivation?
- Do „I my-SELF" wish to do it? Do I express my
higher will, my transpersonal core?

● **What is "WORK"?**

We distinguish two kinds of work:

- I can work to develop my consciousness and myself
or
- I can work in a more economic sense of the word,
which means I DO SOMETHING FOR
SOMEONE ELSE, WHO AGREES WITH THIS.

Work in its common meaning is usually linked to different degrees
of income (to satisfy my needs), to relationships (with co-workers,
customers) and to satisfaction. So it can fulfil more or less my principal needs and avoid my main fears (see above).

Classical view of wage work: POINTS OF VIEWS OF EMPLOYEE and EMPLOYER

MEANINGFULNESS	TEAMWORK & CONTACT WITH CUSTMORS	SALARY (INCOME)

employment

SKILLS (THINK)	PRESENCE (FEEL)	MOTIVATION TO WORK (WILL)

Meditation:

- Working for income usually fulfils more or less the three main personal needs i.e. giving meaning, relationships and money (to survive). Almost everyone works for others for some time every week. Or do you know somebody who doesn't (except the disabled or ill)? They all need an income to carry on living and working for each other. Why don't they all get some money for their efforts?

- Why don't we think separately about the topic of income and the topic of work? Is this usual combination a natural law?

- The economy exists to fulfil each other's needs. It works on the basis of exploitation of nature, human potential, and the labor and creativity of our ancestors. All these three aspects are donated to the living mankind as free gifts. Shouldn't we share this richness to allow everyone to live in dignity?

- Millions of people work directly or indirectly to allow you to purchase a single product. Shouldn't this continue? If so, they all need an income! But how?

4. PERSONAL DAILY PRACTICE:

INDIVIDUAL DEVELOPMENT - "I AM"

4.1 INTEGRAL THREEFOLDING LIVE - THE TETRAHEDRAL MODEL IN ACTION:

THREE TETRAHEDRONS and 12 ASPECTS

SHORT BASIC EXERCISE

(TO DO 6 TIMES IN A CANONICAL WAY:
123456, 234561, 345612, 456123, 561234, 612345)

1. PUT YOUR RIGHT FOOT OUT IN FRONT OF YOU,
    RAISE YOUR RIGHT FOREARM SO YOUR HAND IS
    CLOSE TO YOUR RIGHT SHOULDER AND MAKE A
    FIST, LOOK TO YOUR RIGHT AND SAY "I AM"

2. PUT YOUR RIGHT FOOT TO YOUR RIGHT, RAISE
    YOUR LEFT FOREARM SO YOUR HAND IS CLOSE
    TO YOUR LEFT SHOULDER, (KEEPING YOUR
    RIGHT ARM IN ITS POSITION), LOOK TO YOUR
    LEFT AND SAY "I CAN"

3. RETURN YOUR RIGHT FOOT TO ITS INITIAL PO-
    SITION, KEEP YOUR LEFT ARM IN THE SAME PO-
    SITION AND STRETCH OUT YOUR RIGHT ARM IN
    FRONT OF YOU AND OPEN YOUR RIGHT HAND,
    WITH THE PALM FACING INSIDE, LOOK IN
    FRONT OF YOU AND SAY "I FEEL" (LIKE SHAK-
    ING SOMEONE'S HAND – "RELATIONSHIP")

4. PUT YOUR LEFT FOOT OUT IN FRONT OF YOU, STRETCH OUT YOUR LEFT ARM IN FRONT OF YOU AND OPEN YOUR LEFT HAND, WITH THE PALM FACING INSIDE AND FACING THE PALM OF YOUR RIGHT HAND (KEEP YOUR RIGHT ARM IN ITS LAST POSITION), LOOK UP TO THE SKY AND SAY "I WANT" (LIKE OPENING YOUR ARMS "TO RECEIVE")

5. PLACE YOUR LEFT FOOT TO YOUR LEFT, LOWER YOUR RIGHT ARM TO ITS INITIAL POSITION (KEEPING YOUR LEFT ARM IN ITS LAST POSITION), LOOK DOWN TO THE GROUND AND SAY "I DO" ("BEING ACTIVE ON EARTH")

6. PUT YOUR FEET AND ARMS BACK TO THEIR INITIAL POSITIONS, LOOK IN FRONT OF YOU AND SAY "I SERVE"

===

You can do this exercise early in the morning after waking up, maybe in connection with the 12 postures described below.

The whole exercise finishes with "I DO" (I realize something in this world), a good intention for the rest of the day.

As soon as the exercise becomes routine, change little things each day, like skipping the arm part or the foot part or like changing a word. You also can visualize the exercise in your imagination.

4.2 CONSCIOUS ACTIVITIES FOR SEVEN DAYS

DAILY CONSCIOUSNESS EXERCISE

Each morning, decide on a resolution you intend to execute during the day. As this is a conscious decision of your will, consider this resolution your first priority each day, besides your other obligations and daily routine. The Witness-I will be your companion.

Below you will find suggestions for each day of the week (three for Sundays). Consider them as proposals, not as obligations. You may change the resolution, but be sure to choose an activity covering the same aspect of your being (see map of the human being), as the proposals represent different aspects of an integral human being.

After making your resolution, try to think of it at least once each hour. Take one conscious breath. While inhaling, say inwardly "I", feeling the air coming from above into the middle of your body. While exhaling you say inwardly "AM" feeling the energetic sensation in your whole body.

Also, pay attention to possible physical blockages. You might want to relax three points in your body that are especially susceptible to tension: neck, shoulders and buttocks. You might also be aware of your actual thoughts, feelings, body sensations and needs. How conscious are you of what you are and do?

Before going to sleep in the evening ask yourself: Was my self-awareness active? How many times (hours) did I think to remember my exercise of the day? Did I do it? A good exercise before falling asleep is to remember your whole day but chronologically in reverse.

Supplementary possibilities:

- If you have time in the morning, imagine your day and how you intend to put the exercise into practice. Take note of your feelings, thoughts and sensations.

- In addition to the "I AM" breathing, you could do a second breathing with feeling sensation in the following parts of the body:
  Monday: your face (thinking: liberate your thoughts!)
  Tuesday: your right arm (relations and feelings: empathy)
  Wednesday: your right leg (body: what do I let into my body?)
  Thursday: the back of your head and your spinal column (thinking: hidden potentials?)
  Friday: your left arm (relations and feelings: be peaceful)
  Saturday: your left leg (body: put resolutions into practice!)

- How long can I stay conscious?
  Take one aspect of something your senses assimilate.
  Example 1 : Listening to music and keeping your focus on the guitar.
  Example 2: Sitting in the bus and consciously watching all the road signs.

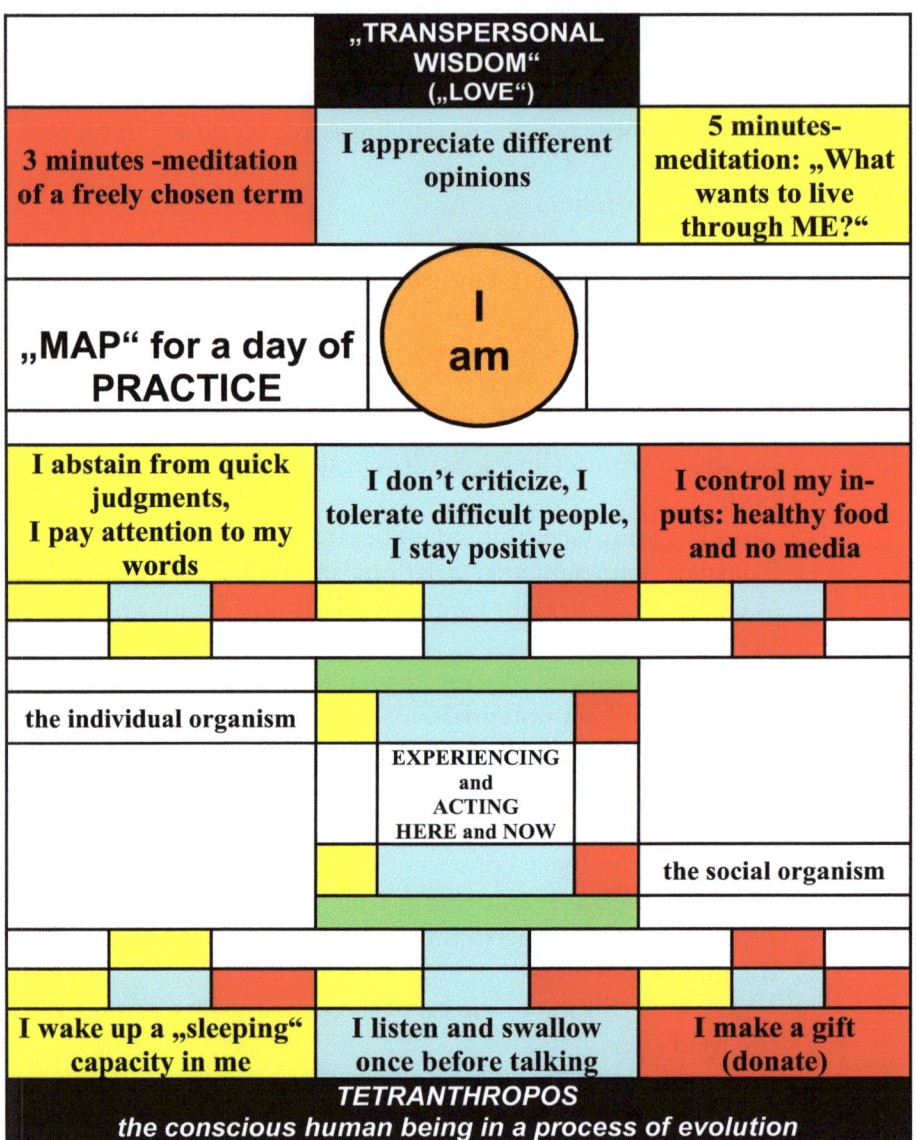

	„TRANSPERSONAL WISDOM" **(„LOVE")**	
3 minutes -meditation of a freely chosen term	**I appreciate different opinions**	**5 minutes- meditation: „What wants to live through ME?"**
„MAP" for a day of PRACTICE	**I am**	
I abstain from quick judgments, I pay attention to my words	**I don't criticize, I tolerate difficult people, I stay positive**	**I control my in- puts: healthy food and no media**
the individual organism	**EXPERIENCING and ACTING HERE and NOW**	
		the social organism
I wake up a „sleeping" capacity in me	**I listen and swallow once before talking**	**I make a gift (donate)**

TETRANTHROPOS
the conscious human being in a process of evolution

86

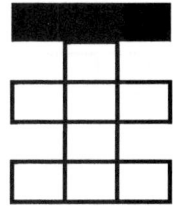

1. I meditate on a freely chosen word (term) for three minutes. (Sunday)

2. I try to perceive different opinions with good humour today. (Sunday)

3. I take at least 5 minutes to meditate on the sentence « What wants to live through ME ? » (Sunday)

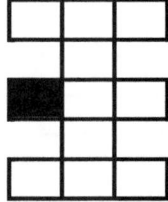

4. I abstain from quick judgments. I try to perceive everything as neutral, as if it were completely new to me. I observe my thoughts and words. (Monday)

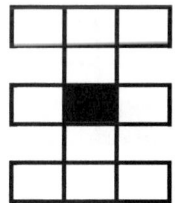

5. I don't criticize anything. I try to tolerate patiently difficult people. I concentrate on the positive aspects of reality. (Tuesday)

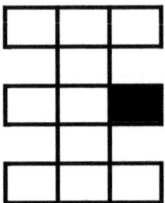

6. I control my inputs. I eat in a healthy way. I don't eat food like cakes, crisps, chocolate or drink alcohol. I only eat a maximum of three meals and nothing in between. I don't read a daily newspa per or magazines. I don't watch TV or listen to any news on the radio. (Wednesday)

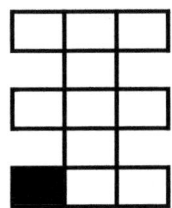

7. I wake up a sleeping capacity in me. I do something useful that I do not normally do. I take an initiative beyond my daily routine. (Thursday)

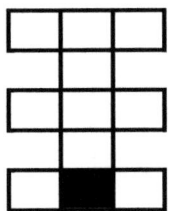

8. Many people talk more than is necessary. I will mainly try to listen today. I swallow once or take a deep breath before talking. (Friday)

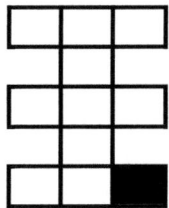

9. I make a gift. (Saturday)

"This body will be taken by death. Before it is taken by death, give it to love. Whatsoever you have will be taken away. Before it is taken away why not share it? That is the only way of possessing it. If you can share and give you are the master. ... If you can give there will be no death. Before anything can be taken away from you, you will have already given it, you will have made it a gift. There can be no death. For a lover there is no death." (My Way: The Way of he White Clouds, Osho)

also see: Charles Eisenstein: www.sacred-economics.com (Sacred Economics traces the history of money from ancient gift economies to modern capitalism, revealing how the money system has contributed to alienation, competition, and scarcity, destroyed community, and necessitated endless growth.)

Simplified alternative:

I DO !

Monday	my mind	I avoid mass media
Tuesday	my relations	I listen empathically
Wednesday	my body	I eat healthy
Thursday	my mind	I am relaxed and humorous
Friday	my relations	I act and react peacefully
Saturday	my body	I move for health
Sunday	my self	I meditate "I AM"

4.3 TWELVE POSTURES - 36 BREATHINGS

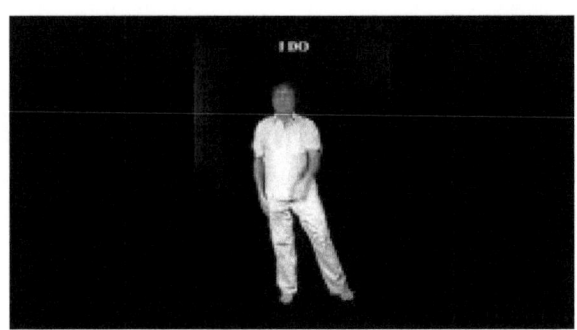

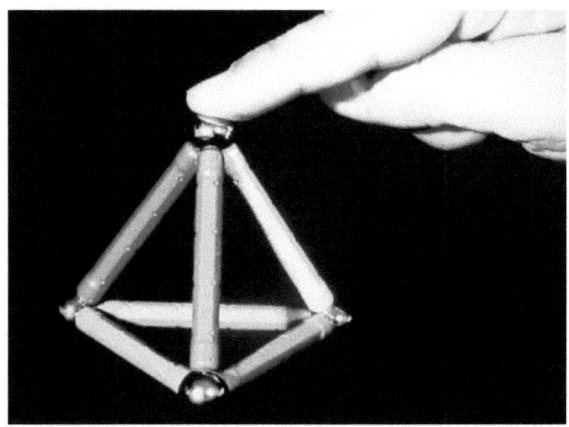

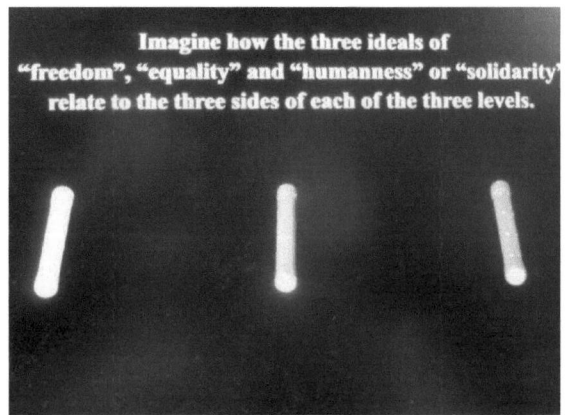

Imagine how the three ideals of "freedom", "equality" and "humanness" or "solidarity" relate to the three sides of each of the three levels.

POSTURES AND
FINGER EXERCISES

VIDEOS
on twelve perspectives
of a Human Being

Videos C. Pauly (2014, in Englisch)

=======

12 perspectives of a human being

https://www.youtube.com/watch?v=UW9yCMLh4gQ

12 perspectives – basic exercise

https://www.youtube.com/watch?v=ij7T8rAwng4

12 perspectives– 12 postures

https://www.youtube.com/watch?v=DHUsfMvriAg

No. 1

LOCATION IN THE MODEL: UPPER TETRAHEDRON -
TRANSPERSONAL: TOP

THEME: "BEING"

PRIVATE LEVEL: MY MEANING OF LIFE
"MANTRA": I AM
QUALITY: NOTHING, EVERYTHING
"EXPLANATION": I AM MY HIGHER BEING AS PART OF
THE ABSOLUTE
COLOUR: WHITE

POSTURE FOR A FOUR-PART BREATH TO REPEAT TWO TIMES:

1. BREATHING IN ("LET COME"): RAISE THE RIGHT ARM HIGH UP, THINKING YOU ARE "ONLINE"("IN LOVE"), CONNECTED WITH THE HIGHEST HIGH AND THE LOWEST LOW (SAY "I").
2. BREATHING OUT ("LET GO"): GO BACK TO THE INITIAL POSITION ("AM").
3. END OF BREATHING OUT COMPLETELY ("SETTLE DOWN"): RELAX.
4. WAITING FOR THE NEXT BREATHING IN TO TAKE PLACE ("BECOMING ONE").

ALTERNATIVE: FINGER EXERCISE (3 TIMES):

1. BREATHING IN ("LET COME"): RAISE THE RIGHT INDEX FINGER, THINKING YOU ARE "ONLINE"("IN LOVE"), CONNECTED WITH THE HIGHEST HIGH AND THE LOWEST LOW (SAY "I").
2. BREATHING OUT ("LET GO"): GO BACK TO YOUR INITIAL POSITION (SAY "AM").
3. AFTER BREATHING OUT COMPLETELY ("SETTLE DOWN"): RELAX.
4. WAITING FOR YOUR NEXT BREATH ("BECOMING ONE").

Karlfried Graf Dürckheim told us that breathing is the innate key movement for transformation. You have to understand that you should not breathe in, but that "it inspires you". This is a gift you receive. The inspiration includes three aspects in the same movement: the opening, the visitation and the fullness. But to be able to receive, you first have to be active: let go, settle down and give everything while breathing out. If you are active while breathing in, you close the door instead of opening it.

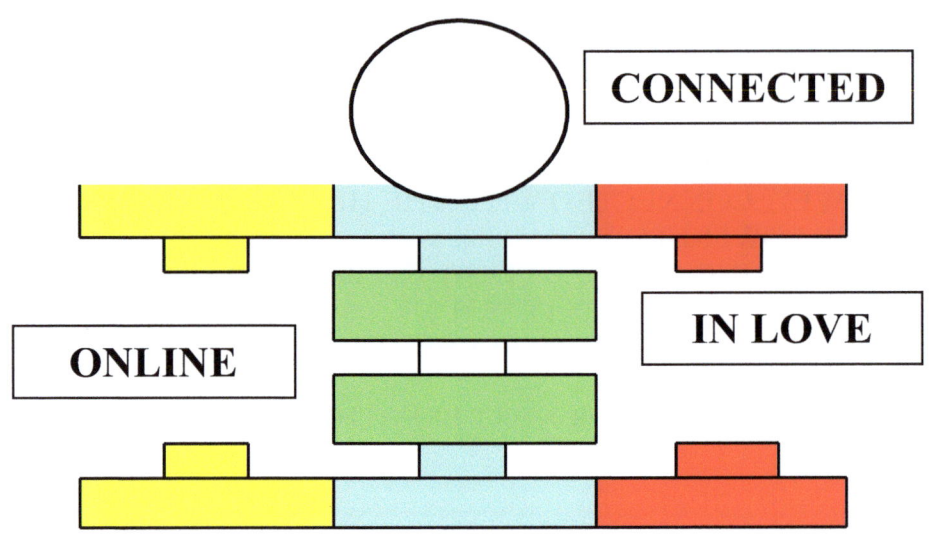

CONNECTED

ONLINE

IN LOVE

No. 2

LOCATION IN THE MODEL: UPPER TETRAHEDRON -
TRANSPERSONAL : BASE

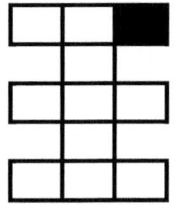

THEME: WILL OF LIFE

PRIVATE LEVEL: I AM A MANIFESTATION OF THE
ABSOLUTE - DEVELOPMENT OF I AM
"MANTRA": I BECOME
QUALITY: FREEDOM
(inverted state compared to the other two tetrahedrons)
"EXPLANATION": THREEFOLDING OF THE ABSOLUTE
- FIRST STEP
FREE UNFOLDING OF THE EMANATION OF REALITY
COLOUR: YELLOW

POSTURE FOR A FOUR-PART BREATHING EXERCISE
TO BE REPEATED TWICE:

1. BREATHING IN: RAISE YOUR LEFT ARM HIGH
   (SAY "I").
2. BREATHING OUT ("LET GO"): GO BACK TO YOUR
   INITIAL POSITION (SAY "BECOME").
3. AFTER BREATHING OUT: COMPLETELY
   ("SETTLE DOWN"): RELAX.
4. AS YOU WAIT FOR YOUR NEXT BREATH ("BECOMING
   ONE").

ALTERNATIVE: FINGER EXERCISE (3 TIMES):

1. BREATHING IN: RAISE YOUR RIGHT INDEX FINGER
   (SAY "I").
2. BREATHING OUT ("LET GO"): LOWER YOUR RIGHT
   INDEX FINGER AND RAISE YOUR LEFT INDEX FINGER
   (SAY "BECOME").
3. AFTER BREATHING OUT COMPLETELY
   ("SETTLE DOWN"): GO BACK TO YOUR INITIAL
   POSITION AND RELAX.
4. AS YOU WAIT FOR YOUR NEXT BREATH
   ("BECOMING ONE").

ACTIVITY OF THE DAY:

DAY OF THE WEEK: SUNDAY
SUGGESTED ACTIVITY No. 1/3: "I take at least 5 minutes to meditate
on the sentence "What wants to live through ME?"
and CONSCIOUSNESS EXERCISE: THINK ONCE EVERY HOUR
OF THE ACTIVITY OF THAT DAY

No. 3

LOCATION IN THE MODEL: UPPER TETRAHEDRON -
TRANSPERSONAL : BASE

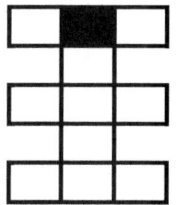

THEME: DIVERSITY (RICHNESS-KINGDOM)

PRIVATE LEVEL: I REALIZE I HAVE AN INFINITE
NUMBER OF CHOICES
"MANTRA": I BREATHE
QUALITY: EQUALITY
"EXPLANATION": THREEFOLDING OF THE ABSOLUTE
-SECOND STEP
EVERYTHING THAT EXISTS HAS THE SAME RIGHT TO
BE
COLOUR: BLUE

POSTURE FOR A FOUR-PART BREATHING EXERCISE TO BE REPEATED TWICE:

1. BREATHING IN: RAISE BOTH ARMS AT A 45° ANGLE TO THE SKY (SAY "I").
2. BREATHING OUT ("LET GO"): GO BACK TO YOUR INITIAL POSITION TOUCHING YOUR STOMACH ON THE WAY (SAY "BREATHE").
3. AFTER BREATHING OUT COMPLETELY ("SETTLE DOWN"): RELAX.
4. AS YOU WAIT FOR YOUR NEXT BREATH ("BECOMING ONE").

ALTERNATIVE: FINGER EXERCISE (3 TIMES):

1. BREATHING IN: RAISE YOUR RIGHT INDEX FINGER (SAY "I").
2. BREATHING OUT ("LET GO"): LOWER THE RIGHT INDEX FINGER AND RAISE ALL FINGERS AT THE SAME TIME (SAY "BREATHE").
3. AFTER BREATHING OUT COMPLETELY ("SETTLE DOWN"): GO BACK TO YOUR INITIAL POSITION AND RELAX.
4. AS YOU WAIT FOR YOUR NEXT BREATH ("BECOMING ONE").

ACTIVITY OF THE DAY:

DAY OF THE WEEK: SUNDAY
SUGGESTED ACTIVITY No. 2/3:
"Today, I will try to appreciate different opinions."
and CONSCIOUSNESS EXERCISE: THINK ONCE EVERY HOUR
OF THE ACTIVITY OF THAT DAY

No. 4

LOCATION IN THE MODEL: UPPER TETRAHEDRON - TRANSPERSONAL : BASE

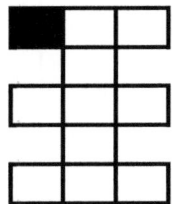

THEME: CREATIVITY (WORD-NAME-IDEAS)

PRIVATE LEVEL: INCARNATION OF THE "I AM"
"MANTRA": I "GROUND"
QUALTY: HUMANNESS
(inverted state compared to the other two tetrahedrons)
"EXPLANATION": THE HUMAN BEING IS CREATED
AND DEVELOPS ON EARTH IN A HUMAN BODY THAT IS
SELF-CREATIVE
COLOUR: RED

POSTURE FOR A FOUR-PART BREATHING EXERCISE TO REPEAT TWICE:

1. BREATHING IN: STAND IN AN UPRIGHT POSITION WITH BOTH LEGS APART AT A 45° ANGLE, KNEES SLIGHTLY BENT. BE CONSCIOUS OF YOUR GROUND ING, i.e. YOUR STANDING ON THE EARTH. FEEL THE ENERGY COMING UP INTO OUR BODY (SAY "I").
2. BREATHING OUT ("LET GO"): LET GO OF ALL YOUR USED ENERGY AND BAD FEELINGS (SAY "GROUND").
3. GO BACK TO THE INITIAL POSITION. AFTER BREATHING OUT COMPLETELY ("SETTLE DOWN"): RELAX.
4. AS YOU WAIT FOR THE NEXT BREATHING IN TO TAKE PLACE ("BECOMING ONE").

ALTERNATIVE: FINGER EXERCISE (3 TIMES):

1. BREATHING IN: RAISE YOUR RIGHT INDEX FINGER (SAY "I").
2. BREATHING OUT ("LET GO"): LOWER YOUR RIGHT INDEX FINGER AND MAKE A FIST (SAY "GROUND").
3. AFTER BREATHING OUT COMPLETELY ("SETTLE DOWN"): GO BACK TO YOUR INITIAL POSITION AND RELAX.
4. AS YOU WAIT FOR THE NEXT BREATHING IN TO TAKE PLACE ("BECOMING ONE").

ACTIVITY OF THE DAY:

DAY OF THE WEEK: SUNDAY
SUGGESTED ACTIVITY No. 3/3:
"I meditate on a freely chosen term for three minutes."
and CONSCIOUSNESS EXERCISE: THINK ONCE EVERY HOUR
OF THE ACTIVITY OF THAT DAY

No. 5

LOCATION IN THE MODEL: MIDDLE TETRAHEDRON - INSIDE (PERSONAL) : TOP

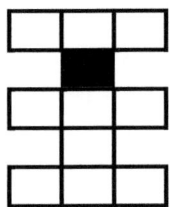

THEME: WITNESS

PRIVATE LEVEL: I AM A SPIRITUAL BEING INCARNAT-
ED IN A HUMAN BODY
"MANTRA": I WITNESS
QUALTY: NEUTRALITY
"EXPLANATION": THE SWELL BETWEEN THE RED OF
CREATIVITY AND THE YELLOW OF HUMAN SKILLS
COLOUR: ORANGE

POSTURE FOR A FOUR-PART BREATHING EXERCISE TO BE REPEATED TWICE:

1. BREATHING IN: STAND STILL, EYES CLOSED, AND FEEL THE AIR COMING DOWN INTO YOUR CHEST (SAY "I").
2. BREATHING OUT ("LET GO"): STAND STILL, FEEL YOUR WHOLE BODY (SAY "WITNESS").
3. AFTER BREATHING OUT COMPLETELY ("SETTLE DOWN"): RELAX.
4. AS YOU WAIT FOR YOUR NEXT BREATH ("BECOMING ONE").

ALTERNATIVE: FINGER EXERCISE (3 TIMES):

1. BREATHING IN: PLACE BOTH HANDS ON YOUR STOMACH, RIGHT HAND OVER YOUR LEFT HAND, EYES CLOSED, AND FEEL THE AIR FILLING YOUR CHEST (SAY "I").
2. BREATHING OUT ("LET GO"): FEEL YOUR WHOLE BODY (SAY "WITNESS").
3. AFTER BREATHING OUT COMPLETELY ("SETTLE DOWN"): GO BACK TO YOUR INITIAL POSITION AND RELAX.
4. AS YOU WAIT FOR YOUR NEXT BREATH ("BECOMING ONE").

No. 6

LOCATION IN THE MODEL: MIDDLE TETRAHEDRON - INSIDE (PERSONAL) : BASE

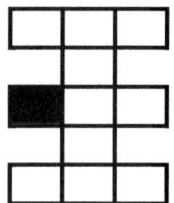

THEME: SKILLS

"EXPLANATION": I HAVE MANY SKILLS THAT I CAN USE FOR MY BENEFIT AND THE BENEFIT OF OTHERS (="WORK") IF I WISH TO
PRIVATE LEVEL: I AM AWARE OF MY SKILLS – I'M A FREE "ARTIST"
"MANTRA": I CAN
QUALTY: FREEDOM
COLOUR: YELLOW

POSTURE FOR A FOUR-PART BREATHING EXERCISE TO BE REPEATED TWICE:

1. BREATHING IN: RAISE YOUR RIGHT ARM TO A 45° ANGLE IN FRONT OF YOUR HEAD (SAY "I").
2. BREATHING OUT ("LET GO"): TOUCH YOUR 'THIRD EYE'. (SAY "CAN").
3. RETURN TO YOUR INITIAL POSITION. AFTER BREATHING OUT COMPLETELY ("SETTLE DOWN"): RELAX.
4. AS YOU WAIT FOR YOUR NEXT BREATH ("BECOMING ONE").

ALTERNATIVE: FINGER EXERCISE (3 TIMES):

1. BREATHING IN: RAISE YOUR RIGHT INDEX FINGER (SAY "I").
2. BREATHING OUT ("LET GO"): LOWER YOUR RIGHT INDEX FINGER AND RAISE YOUR RIGHT THUMB (SAY "CAN").
3. AFTER BREATHING OUT COMPLETELY ("SETTLE DOWN"): GO BACK TO YOUR INITIAL POSITION AND RELAX.
4. AS YOU WAIT FOR YOUR NEXT BREATH ("BECOMING ONE").

ACTIVITY OF THE DAY:

DAY OF THE WEEK: MONDAY
SUGGESTED ACTIVITY: "I abstain from making judgments. I try to perceive everything today as neutral, as if it were completely new to me (non-identification). I watch my thoughts and words (awareness)."
and CONSCIOUSNESS EXERCISE: THINK ONCE EVERY HOUR OF THE ACTIVITY OF THAT DAY

LOCATION IN THE MODEL: MIDDLE TETRAHEDRON -
INSIDE (PERSONAL) : BASE

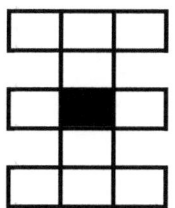

THEME: RELATIONSHIPS

"EXPLANATION": I'M IN MANY RELATIONSHIPS AS A
PRIVATE PERSON, AN EMPLOYEE OR A CITIZEN
PRIVATE LEVEL: I HAVE FEELINGS TOWARDS FAMILY
MEMBERS, FRIENDS, COLLEAGUES, BUT ALSO
TOWARDS NATURE, ANIMALS ...
"MANTRA": I MEET OR I FEEL
QUALTY: EQUALITY
COLOUR: BLUE

POSTURE FOR A FOUR-PART BREATHING EXERCISE TO BE REPEATED TWICE:

1. BREATHING IN: RAISE YOUR LEFT ARM TO A 45°
2. ANGLE BEHIND YOUR HEAD ON ITS LEFT SIDE (SAY "I").
3. BREATHING OUT ("LET GO"): TOUCH YOUR HEART (SAY "MEET OR FEEL").
4. GO BACK TO YOUR INITIAL POSITION. AFTER BREATHING OUT COMPLETELY ("SETTLE DOWN"): RELAX.
5. AS YOU WAIT FOR YOUR NEXT BREATH ("BECOMING ONE").

ALTERNATIVE: FINGER EXERCISE (3 TIMES):

1. BREATHING IN: RAISE YOUR RIGHT INDEX FINGER (SAY "I").
2. BREATHING OUT ("LET GO"): RAISE YOUR MIDDLE FINGER AND KEEP YOUR RIGHT INDEX FINGER RAISED (SAY "MEET OR FEEL").
3. AFTER BREATHING OUT COMPLETELY ("SETTLE DOWN"): GO BACK TO YOUR INITIAL POSITION AND RELAX.
4. AS YOU WAIT FOR YOUR NEXT BREATH ("BECOMING ONE").

ACTIVITY OF THE DAY:

DAY OF THE WEEK: TUESDAY
SUGGESTED ACTIVITY:
"I won't criticize anything. I will try to tolerate difficult people patiently. I will concentrate on the positive aspects of reality."
and CONSCIOUSNESS EXERCISE: THINK ONCE EVERY HOUR OF THE ACTIVITY OF THAT DAY

No. 8

LOCATION IN THE MODEL: MIDDLE TETRAHEDRON -
INSIDE (PERSONAL) : BASE

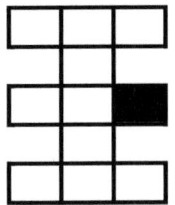

THEME: PHYSICAL NEEDS

"EXPLANATION": TO SURVIVE, I HAVE BASIC
PHYSICAL NEEDS LIKE BREATHING, EATING, DRINK-
ING, WARMTH, SECURITY
PRIVATE LEVEL: IN OUR SOCIETY WE NEED TO BUY
MANY GOODS TO MEET OUR BASIC NEEDS – I'M
DEPENDING ON OTHERS AS THEY DEPEND ON ME
"MANTRA": I NEED OR I WANT
QUALTY: HUMANNESS
COLOUR: RED

POSTURE FOR A FOUR-PART BREATHING EXERCISE
TO BE REPEATED TWICE:

1. BREATHING IN: RAISE YOUR RIGHT ARM IN A 45°

ANGLE BEHIND YOUR HEAD ON ITS RIGHT SIDE
(SAY "I).
2. BREATHING OUT ("LET GO"): TOUCHING YOUR
LOWER BELLY REGION (SAY "NEED OR WANT").
3. GO BACK TO YOUR INITIAL POSITION.
AFTER BREATHING OUT COMPLETELY
("SETTLE DOWN"): RELAX.
4. AS YOU WAIT FOR YOUR NEXT BREATH
("BECOMING ONE").

ALTERNATIVE: FINGER EXERCISE (3 TIMES):

1. BREATHING IN: RAISE YOUR RIGHT INDEX FINGER
(SAY "I").
2. BREATHING OUT ("LET GO"): LOWER THE RIGHT
INDEX FINGER AND RAISE YOUR LITTLE FINGER
(SAY "NEED OR WANT").
3. AFTER BREATHING OUT COMPLETELY
("SETTLE DOWN"): GO BACK TO THE INITIAL
POSITION AND RELAX.
4. AS YOU WAIT FOR YOUR NEXT BREATH
("BECOMING ONE").

ACTIVITY OF THE DAY:

DAY OF THE WEEK: WEDNESDAY
SUGGESTED ACTIVITY:
"I will control my inputs. I will eat healthily. I won't eat things like cakes,
crisps, chocolate or alcohol. I will only eat a maximum of three meals and
nothing in between. I won't read a daily newspaper or magazines. I'll re-
frain from looking at "stupid" things on TV or listening to the news on the
radio."
and CONSCIOUSNESS EXERCISE: THINK ONCE EVERY HOUR OF
THE ACTIVITY OF THAT DAY

No. 9

LOCATION IN THE MODEL: LOWER TETRAHEDRON - OUTSIDE (SOCIAL) : BASE

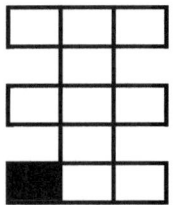

THEME: CULTURE

"EXPLANATION": THE ARTIST PUTS HIS CAPACITIES INTO PRACTICE
PRIVATE LEVEL: LEISURE TIME
"MANTRA": I AM FREE
QUALTY: FREEDOM
COLOUR: YELLOW

POSTURE FOR A FOUR-PART BREATHING EXERCISE TO BE REPEATED TWICE:

1. BREATHING IN: PLACE YOUR LEFT FOOT ONE STEP BACK AND PUT YOUR RIGHT HAND ON THE 'THIRD EYE' (SAY "I").
2. BREATHING OUT ("LET GO"): GO BACK TO YOUR INITIAL POSITION WITH YOUR FOOT (SAY "FREE")
3. GO BACK TO YOUR INITIAL POSITION WITH YOUR HAND. AFTER BREATHING OUT COMPLETELY ("SETTLE DOWN"): RELAX.
4. AS YOU WAIT FOR YOUR NEXT BREATH ("BECOMING ONE").

ALTERNATIVE: FINGER EXERCISE (3 TIMES):

1. BREATHING IN: RAISE YOUR RIGHT INDEX FINGER (SAY "I").
2. BREATHING OUT ("LET GO"): YOUR RIGHT INDEX FINGER TOUCHES YOUR THUMB (SAY "FREE").
3. AFTER BREATHING OUT COMPLETELY ("SETTLE DOWN"): GO BACK TO THE INITIAL POSITION AND RELAX.
4. AS YOU WAIT FOR YOUR NEXT BREATH ("BECOMING ONE").

ACTIVITY OF THE DAY:

DAY OF THE WEEK: THURSDAY
SUGGESTED ACTIVITY:
"I awaken an unused capacity. I do something I can do, but rarely put into practice. I take an initiative beside my daily routine."
and CONSCIOUSNESS EXERCISE: THINK ONCE EVERY HOUR OF THE ACTIVITY OF THAT DAY

No. 10

LOCATION IN THE MODEL: LOWER TETRAHEDRON - OUTSIDE (SOCIAL) : BASE

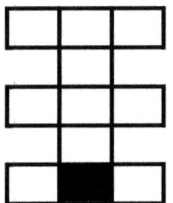

THEME: STATE - LEGISLATION - DEMOCRACY

"EXPLANATION": EACH CITIZEN TALKS TO OTHER PEOPLE INTERESTED IN HIS CAPACITIES, LISTENS TO THEIR NEEDS AND COMMUNICATES HIS NEEDS – A COMMON DECISION IS TAKEN
PRIVATE LEVEL: COMMON DECISIONS IN ONE'S EVERY DAY LIFE
"MANTRA": I COMMUNICATE
QUALITY: EQUAL RIGHTS (DEMOCRACY)
COLOUR: BLUE

POSTURE FOR A FOUR-PART BREATHING EXERCISE TO BE REPEATED TWICE:

1. BREATHING IN: PLACE YOUR RIGHT FOOT ONE

STEP FORWARD TO THE RIGHT (at a 45° ANGLE) AND PLACE YOUR LEFT HAND ON YOUR HEART (SAY "I").

2. BREATHING OUT ("LET GO"):
GO BACK TO YOUR INITIAL POSITION WITH YOUR FOOT (SAY "COMMUNICATE")

3. GO BACK TO YOUR INITIAL POSITION WITH YOUR HAND. AFTER BREATHING OUT COMPLETELY ("SETTLE DOWN"): RELAX.

4. AS YOU WAIT FOR YOUR NEXT BREATH ("BECOMING ONE").

ALTERNATIVE: FINGER EXERCISE (3 TIMES):

1. BREATHING IN: RAISE YOUR RIGHT INDEX FINGER (SAY "I").

2. BREATHING OUT ("LET GO"): LOWER THE RIGHT INDEX FINGER. THE THUMB TOUCHES THE MIDDLE FINGER (SAY "COMMUNICATE").

3. AFTER BREATHING OUT COMPLETELY ("SETTLE DOWN"): GO BACK TO YOUR INITIAL POSITION AND RELAX.

4. AS YOU WAIT FOR YOUR NEXT BREATH ("BECOMING ONE").

ACTIVITY OF THE DAY:

DAY OF THE WEEK: FRIDAY
SUGGESTED ACTIVITY: Practice:
"Many people talk more than necessary. Today, I mainly try to listen. I swallow once or take a deep breath before talking."
and CONSCIOUSNESS EXERCISE: THINK ONCE EVERY HOUR OF THE ACTIVITY OF THAT DAY

No. 11

LOCATION IN THE MODEL: LOWER TETRAHEDRON - OUTSIDE (SOCIAL) : BASE

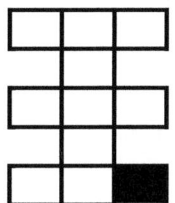

THEME: ECONOMY

"EXPLANATION": THE PRODUCER/CONSUMER PUTS HIS CAPACITIES INTO PRACTICE FOR THE NEEDS OF OTHERS ("WORK")
PRIVATE LEVEL: HELP SATISFY THE NEEDS OF PEOPLE AROUND YOU
"MANTRA": I GIVE (AS A PRESENT)
QUALTY: HUMANNESS ("BROTHERHOOD" – SOLIDARITY)
COLOUR: RED

POSTURE FOR A FOUR-PART BREATHING EXERCISE TO BE REPEATED TWICE:

1. BREATHING IN: WITH YOUR LEFT LEG TAKE ONE STEP FORWARD TO THE LEFT (45° ANGLE) AND PUT YOUR RIGHT HAND ON THE "HARA" (LOWER BELLY) (SAY "I").
2. BREATHING OUT ("LET GO"): GO BACK TO YOUR INITIAL POSITION WITH YOUR FOOT (SAY "GIVE")
3. GO BACK TO YOUR INITIAL POSITION WITH YOUR HAND. AFTER BREATHING OUT COMPLETELY ("SETTLE DOWN"): RELAX.
4. AS YOU WAIT FOR YOUR NEXT BREATH ("BECOMING ONE").

ALTERNATIVE: FINGER EXERCISE (3 TIMES):

1. BREATHING IN: RAISE YOUR RIGHT INDEX FINGER (SAY "I").
2. BREATHING OUT ("LET GO"): LOWER YOUR RIGHT INDEX FINGER, YOUR THUMB TOUCHES YOUR LITTLE FINGER (SAY "GIVE").
3. AFTER BREATHING OUT COMPLETELY ("SETTLE DOWN"): GO BACK TO YOUR INITIAL POSITION AND RELAX.
4. AS YOU WAIT FOR YOUR NEXT BREATH ("BECOMING ONE").

ACTIVITY OF THE DAY:

DAY OF THE WEEK: SATURDAY
SUGGESTED ACTIVITY: "Make a present."
and CONSCIOUSNESS EXERCISE: THINK ONCE EVERY HOUR
OF THE ACTIVITY OF THAT DAY

No. 12

LOCATION IN THE MODEL: LOWER TETRAHEDRON -
OUTSIDE (SOCIAL): TOP

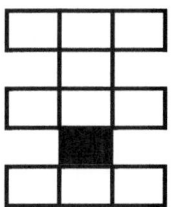

This can also be seen as the top of the unconscious – the reactive
INNER (PERSONAL) TETRAHEDRON of most human beings
in their every day life

UNCONSCIOUS REACTING

THEME: PUT INTO PRACTICE

"EXPLANATION": I ACT CONSCIOUSLY WITH THE
HELP OF MY BODY WHICH IS PART OF NATURE, I TAKE
CONSCIOUS ACTIONS
PRIVATE LEVEL: I TAKE ON RESPONSIBILITIES
"MANTRA": I DO
QUALITY: CONSCIOUSNESS OF MY BODY, SOUL AND
SPIRIT
COLOUR: GREEN

POSTURE FOR A FOUR-PART BREATHING EXERCISE
TO BE REPEATED TWICE:

1. BREATHING IN: WITH YOUR RIGHT FOOT, DRAW ONE
   THIRD OF A CIRCLE IN A DANCE MOVEMENT AND
   MOVE YOUR ARMS AS YOU PLEASE
   (SAY "I").
2. BREATHING OUT ("LET GO"): STOP.
3. AFTER BREATHING OUT COMPLETELY ("SETTLE
   DOWN"): RELAX.
4. AS YOU WAIT FOR THE NEXT BREATH
   ("BECOMING ONE").

ALTERNATIVE: FINGER EXERCISE (3 TIMES):

1. BREATHING IN: RAISE YOUR RIGHT INDEX FINGER
   (SAY "I").
2. BREATHING OUT ("LET GO"): PLAY WITH ALL
   FINGERS (SAY "DO").
3. AFTER BREATHING OUT COMPLETELY ("SETTLE
   DOWN"): GO BACK TO YOUR INITIAL POSITION AND
   RELAX.
4. AS YOU WAIT FOR YOUR NEXT BREATH
   ("BECOMING ONE").

You can replace the last exercise (No. 12) with the following one: Without moving your head move your eyes to the far left and the far right, high up and deep down and finish with rotations of your eyes in every direction.

You can do the 12 postures with only one breath (no repetitions) in addition to the basic exercise. To feel sensation in your body it is good doing this after getting up in the morning. The same is of course possible for the finger exercise during periods waiting or during a boring meeting.

MANTRAS FOR THE POSTURES

("DANCE of the TETRAHEDRON")

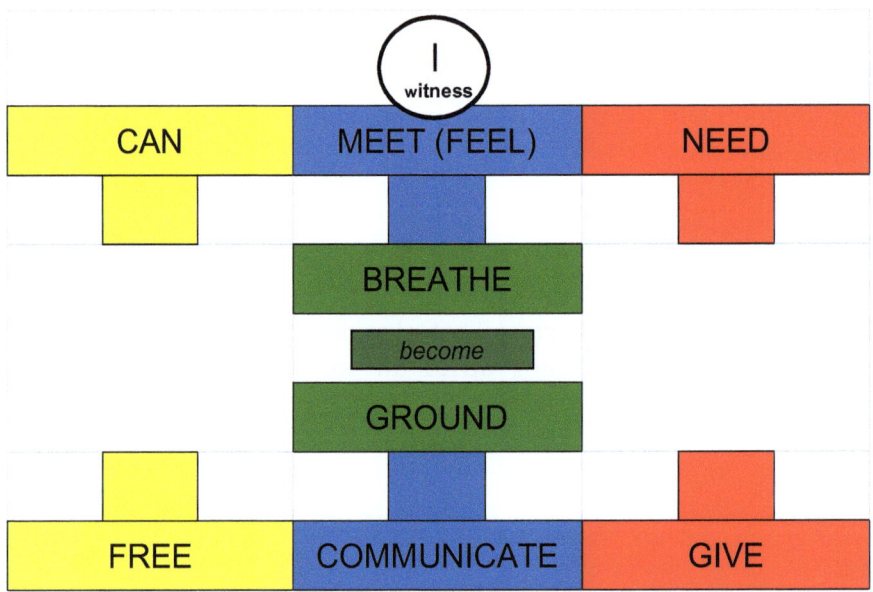

5. THE DEVELOPMENT OF SOCIETY

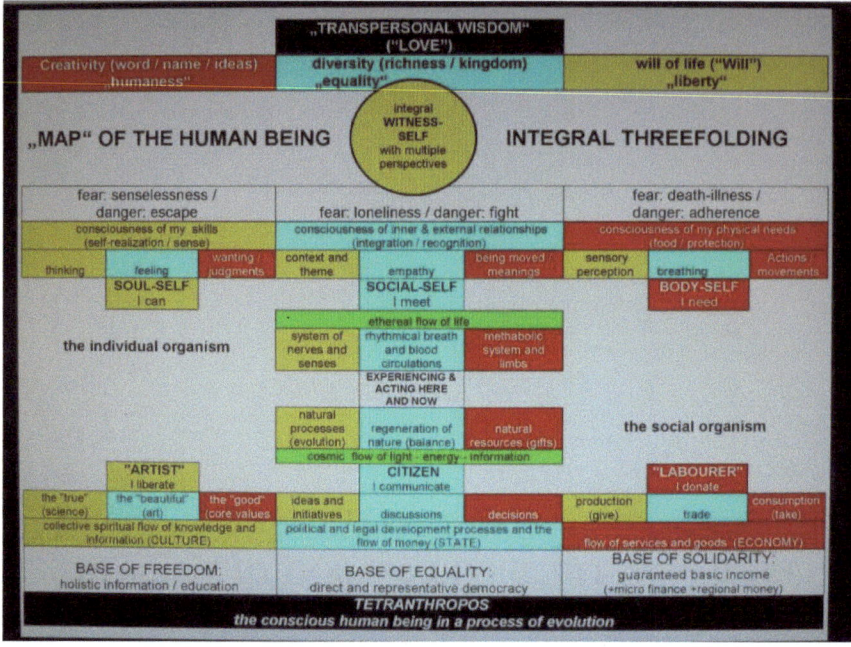

Remember the two-dimensional view of the human being.

His harmonious inclusion in society, including all his aspects, is the main objective of the following chapters.

We continue with two simplified views of the human being in society and a map with a possible perspective of society.

	the "ABSOLUTE"		
"creativity"	"diversity"	"will of life"	
	the conscious "witness"		
thoughts / potentials	feelings / relationships	needs / impulses	
	actions		
creations / culture	communications / state	works / economy	

I inside	I outside
My personal wisdom and evolution; personal development	Individual actions; the work done for other human beings
The culture, information, values, education I share in	The process of state laws and economic activities I share in
WE inside	**WE outside**

I inside	I outside	
self-awareness I witness *("I think")*	*I communicate* *I vote* *("I feel")*	*I give (work)* *I take* *(consume)* *("I want")*
collective awareness *(culture)*		

WE inside

self-awareness I witness **SENSE** *("I think")*	*I communicate* *I vote* **INCLUSION / PEACE** *("I feel")*	*I give (work)* *I take (consume)* **HEALTH** *("I want")*
	We relate *(communicate)* *STATE*	*We produce - we consume* *(cooperate)* *ECONOMY*
collective awareness *CULTURE*	depreciating interest free **REGIONAL MONEY** **- PURCHASE MONEY -** *(+ Euros)*	worldwide **UNCONDITIONAL** **BASIC INCOME** **- GIFT MONEY** to be able to work - *(+ complementary income)* **MICROFINANCE** **- LOAN MONEY without** **interest to promote** **creativity -** and „Social Enterprise" *(+ bank credits)*
	SIMPOL *(simultaneous politics)* **and DIRECT/PARTICIPATORY** **DEMOCRACY** *(+ representative democracy)*	**SOCIAL** **and SOLIDARITY** **ECONOMY** *(associative economics)* **COMMON WELFARE** **BALANCE**
consciousness liberty creativity	democracy equal rights diversity	solidarity humanness will of life

Search for classical definitions and then deliberate terms like:

- Culture, sense of life, health, income
- State, inclusion, peace, democracy, money (purchase money, gift money, loan money), capital (money or human skills and natural resources?)
- Economy (to satisfy each other's needs or to make money?), work (with or without payment?)

What is your DEFINITION? Before using these terms in a discussion, check that you agree on the definition of the main TERMS. Otherwise you may agree superficially, but disagree in fact. This can lead to all sorts of conflicts. Also, deliberate the connections of these terms.

For example "WORK" and "INCOME": Almost every one works regularly for other people, even if some people might work more hours than others. But not everyone gets an income for his work. Why is some work paid and some unpaid? There is enough money and work available, but we have a problem with the fair distribution of money. How can we best assure that everyone gets an income to live on? In former times farmers worked directly for themselves and their family. In a modern economy most people work to satisfy the needs of others. An unconditional basic income could free you for work (see p. 191ff.)! Don't forget we wrote that the richness of nature, the diversity of our human potential, and the result of the labor of our ancestors are granted for free.

What is an "ECONOMY"? And what is its main purpose? Is it to satisfy the needs of human beings, via their cooperation in an economic network? Or is it making financial profits through rivalry and to the detriment of others? Are salaries expenses or part of the profit (profit shares)? What is a healthy or a pathological economy?

SOUL-SELF	SOCIAL-SELF	BODY-SELF
CULTURE (civil society)	STATE	ECONOMY
FREEDOM	EQUAL RIGHTS	HUMANNESS (solidarity)
CONSCIOUSNESS	PEACE	HEALTH

Freedom, equal rights and humanness related to the three main areas
of society. Do you agree?
Consciousness, peace and health are main goals to achieve!

Rudolf Steiner, the initiator of the idea of three-folding the social
organism, said that in the development of humanity, one does not
have the right to feel oneself to be an individual, if one doesn't at the
same time feel oneself a member of the whole of humankind. (Ox-
ford, August 29, 1922 "The Human Being Within the Social Order:
Individual and Society")

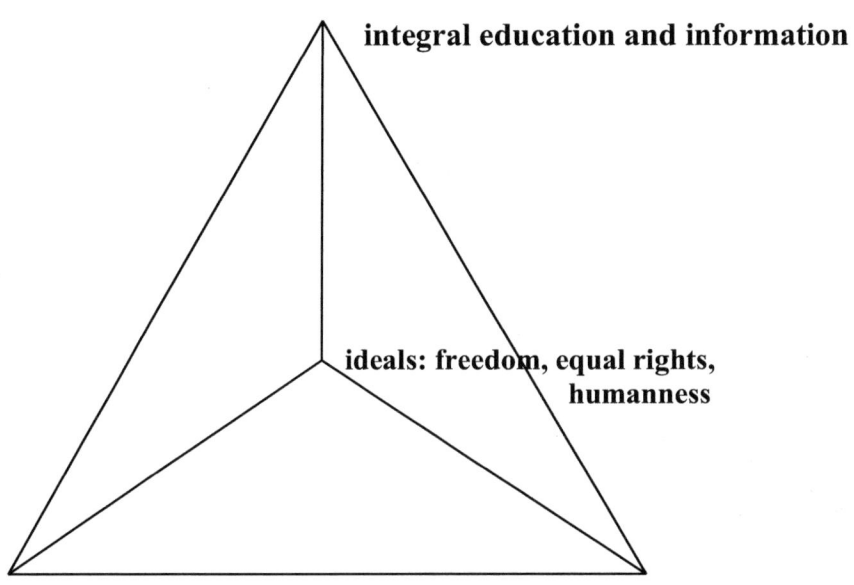

integral education and information

ideals: freedom, equal rights, humanness

direct democracy
(citizens' initiatives and referenda, freedom of information...)

money for economy
unconditional basic income (gift), microcredits
(loan) and regional money (purchase)

"To truly know the world, look deeply within your own being; to truly know yourself, take real interest in the world." (Rudolf Steiner)

Some ideas concerning the development of society will follow.

5.1 EDUCATION and INFORMATION - FREEDOM

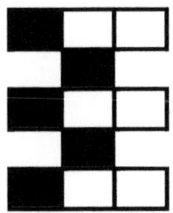

CREATIVITY , the SOUL - SELF (think, feel, want) and the "ARTIST"

I am FREE to be creative and use my skills as an "artist" and I put them into practice: I CAN; I LIBERATE my potentials! This gives me the possibility of self-realization and a purpose to my life.

How can CULTURE support every human being to achieve this?

- The possibility of a lifelong, integral, freely-chosen education (free schools, education vouchers)
- Free access to information of all kinds (internet, media, libraries, permanent education, training courses, lectures) with a maximum of independence from money, state regulation and economic constraints
- A maximum of transparency
- A free press
- No intellectual property
- Supporting self-governance
- Understanding integral threefolding

I am conscious of my potential and my skills and I develop them	I do "liberate" my potentials, meaning I use them practically with a visible result
Culture supports my efforts to develop my potentials and put them into practice	I am creative individually or in a group and share the results of the effort with others

Otto Scharmer shows in his "Theory U" (www.presencing.com) how groups and organizations can develop seven leadership capacities so as to create a future that otherwise would not be possible. His theory possesses similarities with what is said here (the observing witness, connecting to the inner source, creativity/create, act ...).

"When leaders develop the capacity to come near to that source, they experience the future as if it were "wanting to be born" - an experience called "presencing." That experience often carries with it ideas for meeting challenges and for bringing into being an otherwise impossible future. Theory U shows how that capacity for presencing can be developed. ...

Seven Theory U Leadership Capacities.
The journey through the U develops seven essential leadership capacities.

1. Holding the space of listening.
The foundational capacity of the U is listening. Listening to others. Listening to oneself. And listening to what emerges from the collective. Effective listening requires the creation of open space in which others can contribute to the whole.

2. Observing.
The capacity to suspend the "voice of judgment" is key to moving from projection to true observation.

3. Sensing.
The preparation for the experience at the bottom of the U - presencing - requires the tuning of three instruments: the open mind, the open heart, and the open will. This opening process is not passive but an active "sensing" together as a group. While an open heart allows us to see a situation from the whole, the open will enables us to begin to act from the emerging whole.

4. Presencing.
The capacity to connect to the deepest source of self and will allows the future to emerge from the whole rather than from a smaller part or special interest group.

5. Crystalizing.
When a small group of key persons commits itself to the purpose and outcomes of a project, the power of their intention creates an energy field that attracts people, opportunities, and resources that make things happen. This core group functions as a vehicle for the whole to manifest.

6. Prototyping.
Moving down the left side of the U requires the group to open up and deal with the resistance of thought, emotion, and will; moving up the right side requires the integration of thinking, feeling, and will in the context of practical applications and learning by doing.

7. Performing.
... [Organizations] need to convene the right sets of players (frontline people who are connected through the same value chain) and to engage a social technology that allows a multi-stakeholder gathering to shift from debating to co-creating the new." (Otto Scharmer, www.ottoscharmer.com)

Literature: Leading from the Emerging Future: From Ego-System to Eco-System Economics (Otto Scharmer and Katrin Kaufer, 2013)

"We must strive for FREEdom if we strive for self-knowledge."

(Georg I. Gurdjieff)

"The-Earth-Is-Equally-FREE-For-All."

(Georg I. Gurdjieff, All and Everything, First Series)

"It can be argued that the distinction between <u>states</u> and <u>structures</u> of consciousness is one of the most important contributions to the religious dialogue in centuries, and will certainly play a fundamental role in the future of spirituality on this planet. Mastery of the various <u>states of consciousness</u> (e.g. gross, subtle, causal, and non-dual) determines the amount of <u>freedom</u> you can experience in this lifetime, which can be called 'horizontal enlightenment', while development through the many <u>structures of consciousness</u> (e.g. magic, mythic, rational, postmodern, and integral) will determine the degree of <u>fullness</u> you can experience, known as 'vertical enlightenment'. To be fully enlightened you must therefore be both FREE and full, and by recognizing these 'two kinds of higher' you will greatly enhance the amount of warmth, light, and consciousness you have to share with the rest of the world." (

(Ken Wilber)

"Our highest endeavour must be to develop FREE human beings who are able of themselves to impart purpose and direction to their lives. The need for imagination, a sense of truth, and a feeling of responsibility—these three forces are the very nerve of education."

(Rudolf Steiner)

"Therefore the law of a growing inner FREEdom is that which will be most honoured in the spiritual age of mankind."

(Sri Aurobindo)

"A human being is part of the whole called by us the universe, a part limited in time and space. He experiences himself, his thoughts and feelings as something separate from the rest, a kind of optical delusion of his consciousness. This delusion is a kind of prison for us, restricting us to our personal desires and to affection for a few persons nearest to us. Our task must be to FREE ourselves from this prison by widening our circle of compassion to embrace creatures and the whole of nature in its beauty."

(Albert Einstein)

5.2 DEMOCRACY and MONEY -

INTEGRAL POLITICS and EQUAL RIGHTS

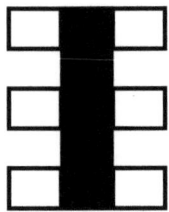

DIVERSITY, the SOCIAL - SELF and the CITIZEN

I am a citizen who benefits from equal rights in a democratic country. I can express my ideas and take initiatives. I can meet other citizens and make proposals for the collective wealth and a harmonious living together. I can enjoy the richness of diversity and I am part of a transparent discussion and decision-making process: I MEET and I COMMUNICATE.

This gives me the possibility of feeling fully included in society, respected and appreciated, avoiding the fear of exclusion.

How can the STATE support the equal inclusion of every citizen in the law-making process and the implementation of these laws?

- Allowing a participatory democracy
- Regulating the process of proposing laws by citizens and civil society with fair criteria, a balanced discussion and a binding decision by the voters (initiative, petition, decision)
- Taking a world-centric view and supporting simultaneously-implemented international policies initiated by civil society

- Making possible binding referenda about new laws emanating from parliament
- Fighting corruption
- Fighting secret lobbying
- Minimising bureaucracy
- Respecting the principle of subsidiarity
- Being responsible for the framing of culture and the economy, but not intervening in these domains
- Regulating the emission and flow of money for the equal well-being of all citizens (avoid compound interest, allow regional moneys that guarantee the flow of money, severely tax speculation that doesn't support the regular economy, tax consumption not wages, ensure the transparency of bank transactions)

I am conscious of my inner (sub-personalities) and outer relationships	**I have a feeling of mutual dependency, I listen and I communicate my points of view**
The state guarantees democracy and ensures equal rights and chances for all	**Participation in a process of evolution of society to a higher level of common development**

Democracy International - Foundation meeting Council, 6 May 2013 - Democracy initiatives from Austria, Belgium, Germany, Luxembourg and the Netherlands are the first members of the Council.

Links: http://www.democracy-international.org
http://www.iri-europe.org

LIVING IN SOCIETY: CULTURE, STATE and ECONOMY

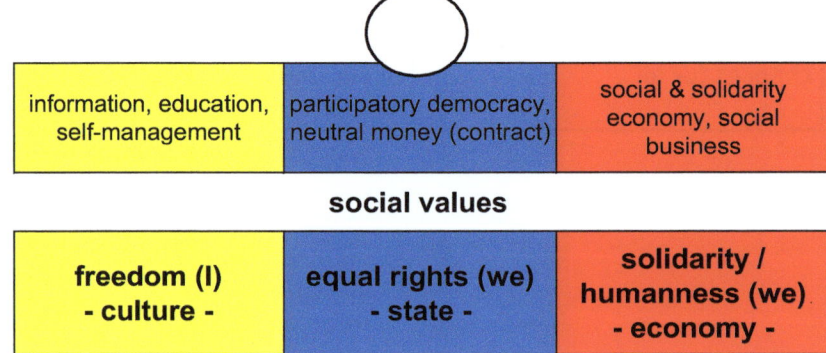

information, education, self-management	participatory democracy, neutral money (contract)	social & solidarity economy, social business
social values		
freedom (I) - culture -	**equal rights (we) - state -**	**solidarity / humanness (we) - economy -**

138

Concerning the topic of democracy and the values of the French revolution, Johannes Stüttgen wrote the following in an article entitled "The Artistic Concept and a Cleansing (Revolution) of Terms". (Paris 1994 - http://www.democracy-in-motion.eu/en/idea/concept/)

1. In the most sublime conceptual image of humankind,

LIBERTY   EQUALITY   FRATERNITY

the principle of the DEMOCRACY is represented by its central element, EQUALITY.
DEMOCRACY is derived from the EQUALITY of all people before the law. The idea of EQUALITY, the central element, does not mean that all people are the same, but only that all have Equal Rights.
Thus, EQUALITY refers to the legal structure of society.
The societal legal structure based on EQUALITY is called DEMOCRACY.

2. Whence, then, is law derived? DEMOCRACY means that "all power stems from the people."

In a DEMOCRACY, the people are the sovereign of the law. But all of us, each one of us, are the people! Each with his or her own voice, and every voice weighs the same. However, this equal weight of every voice is only ensured if each voice is also free, i.e. not pre-empted, not dictated. Here, the first element of the three, LIBERTY, appears. LIBERTY is thus based on the human being as an individual, as a self. It refers to the individual's special features, uniqueness, productivity, and creativity, to what he or she thinks, feels and wants, to the spirit. "Every person is an artist," Joseph Beuys said. He meant the Essence of LIBERTY as the potential of every human being. That is the basis for everything.

Thus, the production and the design of Law, and at a higher level, the production and the design of DEMOCRACY, in which law is based on the principle of the EQUALITY of all before the law, is an individual act of creation by a free person. Rights cannot be created from above, but only from below, i.e. out of the LIBERTY and self-determination of every single human self.

Hence, EQUALITY does not abolish the LIBERTY of the individual, but rather lifts up that LIBERTY to a higher form – the form of the structure of liberty of society.

	We relate (communicate) STATE	We produce - We consume (cooperate) ECONOMY

WE outside (1)

3. However, the highest form of the LIBERTY appears in the third element, FRATERNITY.

FRATERNITY (love) refers to the cooperation of all based on a division of labour in production, circulation, fulfilment of needs and loving, hence careful management of nature and resources. FRATERNITY (love) is the principle of economy implemented by people. It refers to, and brings forth, the future form of a free world with an ecological economy. - Joseph Beuys: "The Social Sculpture"

For this future form, which is to overcome the present not yet free, not yet democratic, not yet fraternal (but rather egotistical) form, the formation of the central element is the decisive threshold step for the realization of real democracy at the end of the 20th century.

For new economic laws, new capital laws, new financial laws derived from the LIBERTY of the human self and its creativity, can be realized only through legal agreements which are democratic, which means based on equal rights.

Thus, the realization of EQUALITY (democracy) from LIBERTY (the creative power of the human self) is the condition for the realization of a FRATERNITY (the Gesamtkunstwerk "Social Sculpture,") in which LIBERTY can fully emerge for the first time."

	Depreciating interest free **REGIONAL MONEY** *PURCHASE MONEY* *(+ Euros)*	worldwide **UNCONDITIONAL BASIC INCOME** *GIFT MONEY* *to be able to work* *(+ complementary income)* --- **MICROFINANCE** *LOAN MONEY* *without interest to pro-* *mote creativity and* *„Social Enterprise"* *(+ bank credits)*

WE Outside (2)

Let's talk about money now and its link to democracy. According to the Wikipedia's definition democracy is a form of government in which all eligible citizens participate equally—either directly or through elected representatives—in the proposal, development, and creation of laws." Money derives its value by being declared to be a legal tender by a government. So it must be accepted as a form of payment within the boundaries of the country, for all debts, public and private. This means that creating a currency is a democratic act.

142

We can distinguish, purchase, loan and gift money. Normally the first thing that comes to mind if we think about money, is that we need it to purchase goods and services. *"Most of the time we are apt to consider money as a single static entity, and not see that it, like all things to do with the social life of mankind, has a rhythm, a life process. We can describe these, by looking at how we ourselves use money. We need money to maintain our physical presence and existence. Buying (purchasing) to meet our needs stimulates the production of goods. We do this rightly from an egocentric viewpoint and it could be described as akin to a metabolic process. After that aspect is to a degree satisfied, we then see that it is more economical to have one person specializing in a particular activity, than to have all of us doing a bit of everything. To make it possible usually means loaning money or contracting in some form the work, and here we lift up ourselves to consider others from a realm of feeling. Loans/contracts help make human labour possible. If we have money over and above this, it has become free of commitments. It is then free for creative activity, free to be 'gifted', and here we enter the realm of altruism. If gifted rightly it goes towards helping bring into being something new, usually helping to set up that which leads towards the purchase of the needs of that new initiative, thereby transforming into purchase money again and creating a healthy cycle and flow of money."* (Anthroposophical Society in New Zealand).

The flow of money is a critical aspect if a community decides to create a regional currency (complementary currency, local currency). This PURCHASE MONEY enables the community to more fully utilize its existing productive resources, which has a catalytic effect on the rest of the local economy. If it operates with a negative interest rate (demurrage), it will circulate much more rapidly than national currencies. The same amount of currency in circulation is re-employed many times and results in far greater overall economic activity. A negative interest rate encourages people to spend the money more quickly. The created wealth stays in the region, since no "rich stranger" takes money out of the local circuit through interest and interest on interest.

Links: http://www.youtube.com/watch?v=BU5CKfju1ss
    http://projects.exeter.ac.uk/RDavies/arian/local.html

A bus called „Omnibus für direkte Demokratie" (http://www.omnibus.org) is driving through Germany to inform people about the ways and chances of direct democracy through discussions and all kinds of action (for example trying to create the possibility of legislative processes initiated by citizens). The "Omnibus" recognises the connection of the topic of democracy with the topic of perception of money as essential for the development of our society (for example, the creation of a democratic credit bank). In the scope of the „study group money" a deliberation took place on how to infuse the way we use money with a new essence stemming from citizens. And one of the most known regional moneys in Europe, the „Chiemgauer", was explained by some of its members (http://en.wikipedia.org/wiki/Chiemgauer   - http://www.youtube.com/watch?v=6_Bf85tX9YE). The work of the "Omnibus" is influenced by Joseph Beuys, who said the following about money in a discussion held on 29 November 1984 at The Meeting House in Ulm, Germany:

"If we want to achieve a different society where the principle of money operates equitably, if we want to abolish the power money has historically gained over people, and position money in relationship to freedom, equality and fraternity – in other words develop a functional view of the interaction between the three great strata or spheres of social forces: the spiritual life, the rights life, and the economic life – then we must elaborate a concept of culture and a concept of art where every person must be an artist in this realm of social sculpture or social art or social architecture – never mind what terms you use. Once people have developed these imaginative concepts – which may come into focus a bit more this evening – having drawn them from their own minds, their recognition and knowledge, but also their feelings and willpower - from the moment they possess them, people will also understand that they are the sovereigns of a state-like whole, and that it is they who formulate the economic laws which will allow money to be freed from its pre-

144

sent characteristics, from the power it exerts because — and by saying this I'm already making a statement about money — it has evolved in the economic context as part of the economic life and is now a commodity. They will recognize, then, that they can free money from being a commodity and that it must become a regulating factor in the rights domain. People will increasingly see that money today is a commodity, in other words, an economic value — I'm trying to say something tangible about money here — that it is an economic value and that we have to reach a stage where it must become a necessary potential, must act as a <u>rights document</u>* for all the creative processes of human work ... ."

* "The precise meaning of this term is open to interpretation. In the further course of the debate, the concept is explained as something that money already partially does: an entitlement to goods and services. However, Beuys seems to use it to signify a broader entitlement to human creativity and dignity: a right to make full use of one's creative potential as both consumer and producer. Later in the debate, Beuys states in clarification (page 32): "*Both sectors, production as well as consumption, must be regulated by democracy which itself has to relate to money. If democracy is not related to money, all the people's democratic efforts will be destroyed by the power money can assume. So unless money has become a full rights document in which the production sector and the consumption sector are embedded in our society, it will continue to ensure the decline of human creativity, of the human soul, of the power of human creation, and the life of nature!*" (Editor's note)

(What is money?: a discussion, Joseph Beuys, 2010, pages 16 and 17)

	SIMPOL (simultaneous politics) and DIRECT / PARTICIPATORY DEMOCRACY (+ representative democracy)	SOCIAL and SOLIDARITY ECONOMY (associative economics) COMMON WELFARE BALANCE

WE ouside (3)

Democracy these days surely isn't related to money in Beuys's sense, but rather to the global speculation which represents a vicious circle of Destructive International Competition that threatens our "democracies".

SIMPOL ("The Simultaneous Policy") is a movement with a world-centric view (global humanity) and a democratic approach (ideas from civil society), which aims to break this vicious circle.

The "Peace and Collaborative Development Network" interviewed John Bunzl, the founder of the "International Simultaneous Policy Organization", on August 13th 2012. They asked him about the problems globalization has brought. This is what he replied:

"... You see, globalization is actually a vicious circle because of capital that moves freely around the globe. Because of that, governments are now stuck in a vicious circle, or a straight jacket, in which they can't actually regulate to solve any of our global problems for fear that investment and jobs will move elsewhere.

So you have a situation where global problems are getting worse and it's not a question that we don't know about them; it's not a question of ignorance. Take global warming, for example. ... The problem is that no nation wants to move first because each fears that dramatic cuts to its emissions will increase the costs to its industries and that will make them uncompetitive with industries elsewhere. So of course no nation acts. So it's not surprising that very little happens.

That's why we have global problems dramatically worsening and yet the governmental response to them is manifestly failing. So, for me, all problems like poverty, global warming, the financial system, corporate power, the out of control media, all of them are really only secondary. Because, to solve any or all of them, you need global cooperation. You need to overcome the vicious circle of destructive competition between governments which prevents them from acting—that's the key issue we have to solve. Solve that vicious circle and you unlock a solution to all the other issues. That's my view anyhow ."

Literature: Global Domestic Politics - A Citizen's Guide to Running a Diverse Planet (J.Bunzl, 2013)

"Simpol invites citizens around the world to use their votes in a completely new way to encourage politicians to solve global problems like global warming, financial market regulation, environmental destruction, war, and social injustice.

Simpol offers us a way to take action on global problems; problems individual governments cannot resolve by acting alone.

That's because these problems cross national boundaries, and because competition between governments to attract investment and jobs means the markets - not the people - end up calling the shots.

Governments cannot act alone to solve these problems because any government doing so would make its economy uncompetitive, leading to inflation, unemployment, or even economic collapse. Any government that moved first would lose out! While governments remain stuck, it's the markets that continue to run politics - not we, the people.

Simpol aims to break this vicious circle by encouraging people around the world to oblige their politicians and governments to cooperate globally in implementing appropriate policies simultaneously for the good of all.

Only by implementing policies simultaneously can our problems be resolved in a way that no nation, corporation, or citizen loses out to its peers. Only by acting globally and simultaneously can governments regain control over global markets. If all nations act together, everybody wins.

Simultaneous implementation would ensure that no country became uncompetitive as a result of pursuing policies that were right for the planet and which embodied our higher aspirations. But politicians will not act together globally unless we make them!

The vicious circle in the economy

"Race to the bottom" is a socio-economic term used to describe a relationship between countries, states, provinces or territories that is an outcome of globalization, free trade, neoliberalism or economic deregulation. The relationship occurs when competition increases between geographic areas over a particular sector of trade and production and when governments are given increased incentive to cut business regulations, labor standards, environmental laws and business taxes. (source: Wikipedia)

By supporting Simpol you are taking politics back! You are telling politicians you'll be voting in future national elections, not for a particular candidate or party, but for ANY candidate or party, within reason, who has signed the Simpol Pledge; a declaration of support for a process leading to the simultaneous implementation of a range of policies to solve global problems. Or, if you have a party preference, your support signifies you want your preferred party to make that Pledge.

In that way, you still retain the ultimate right to vote as you please. But you are also clearly indicating to politicians that you'll be giving strong preference to those who have signed the Pledge, to the exclusion of those who haven't. With many parliamentary seats, and even entire national elections, hanging on a relatively low number of votes, even a relatively small block of Simpol supporters can make it in the vital interests of politicians to sign the Pledge. This is the simple mechanism Simpol supporters use to advance our cause. It's the simple mechanism we're using to take politics back.

Simpol's approach is peaceful, open, democratic, and it's free. By supporting Simpol, you gain the opportunity to

- *contribute, if you wish, to the formulation of specific policies to solve global problems, and*
- *you join with others to use your vote in a new and effective way to drive the politicians of all parties and countries to implement those policies together."* (http://simpol.org)

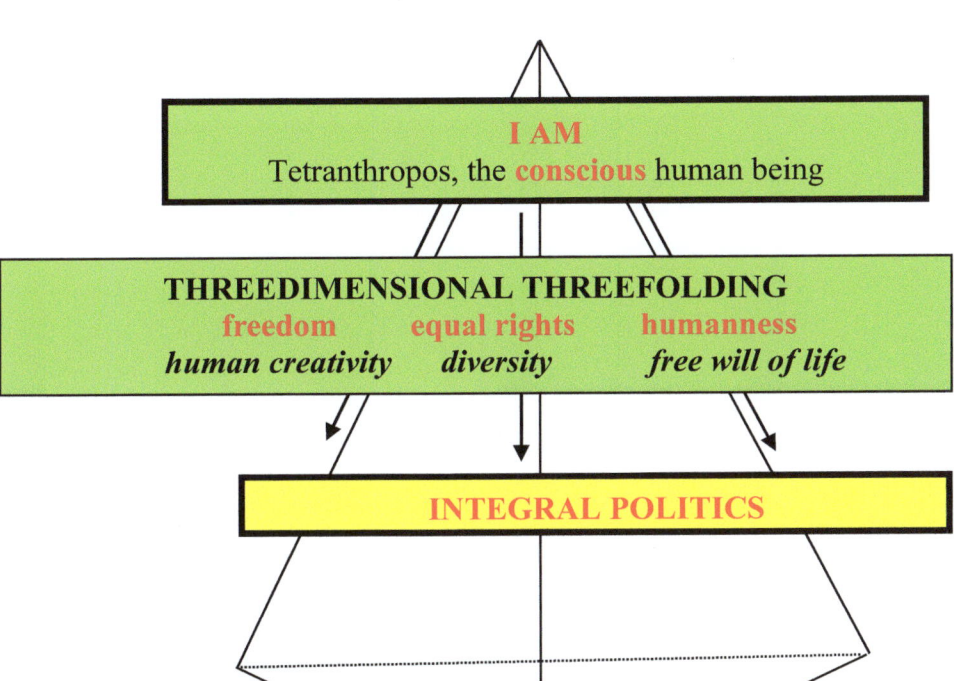

I AM
Tetranthropos, the **conscious** human being

THREEDIMENSIONAL THREEFOLDING

| freedom | equal rights | humanness |
| *human creativity* | *diversity* | *free will of life* |

INTEGRAL POLITICS

TRANSPERSONAL
Free flow of information for multiple perspectives as a basis for a self-determined integral daily life
(*routine past-centred and creative future-centred WORK*)

UNCONDITIONAL
Unconditional Basic Income, Regional Currencies and Credits free of interest as a basis for an "Economy of the Common Good"
(*make and get presents*)

WORLDCENTRIC
Direct Democracy as a basis for Simultaneous Policy
(*poverty reduction, ecology, democratic money …*)

"Integral Politics" for the future?

We close this chapter with the question "What is meant by Integral Politics". Integral Politics take into account all perspectives and start from a worldcentric perspective. They enhance the promotion of individual and collective development. They encourage the interaction of a personal and transpersonal culture of consciousness with the democratic affairs of society and the financial affairs of the economy. They open their horizon for all kinds of different views in an empathic manner.

5.3 WORK and ASSOCIATIVE, SOCIAL and SOLIDARITY ECONOMY - HUMANNESS

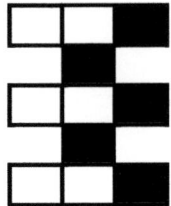

WILL OF LIFE, the BODY - SELF and the WORKER/CONSUMER

"Life" or the will of life is encountered by every one. I am free to follow the flow of life or go against it and impose my will in the circumference of my limited possibilities. As a human being I need life and life needs me. One of my constraints in order to survive is my needs, especially my physical needs (water, food, air, heat, security ...). These are the conditions for all my fellow humans. We need one another and we are probably much more interrelated than we are conscious of. Our modern economy is built on the basis of working for one another. I give ("worker") and I take ("consumer"). Everyone has skills. They are all of value to "the Whole": I NEED and I GIVE.

How can the ECONOMY support humanness and solidarity so that it satisfies the needs of all human beings?

- Make possible the distribution of an unconditional basic income for every human being to give him/her the chance to participate with his/her skills in the economic process.
- Think of the notions of work and income separately - everyone needs both.
- Support the idea of social entrepreneurship (importance of stakeholder values).
- Make it possible for entrepreneurs to have access to credits and micro-credits (for example in regional money free of interest).
- Support an open culture (innovation, research, education).
- Enhance the flow of services and goods to disadvantaged areas.

I am conscious of my needs, especially physical needs	I work and give my potentials
Economy with the goal of meeting the basic needs of every human being	We work for one another, because giving is satisfying

Let's talk about money again. First of all of GIFT MONEY in form of an unconditional basic income, which gives everyone the possibility of an INCOME and the possibility to WORK, which means to do something for other people.

A problem is that in our society work normally means working for other people and receiving money as a reward (wage work). But according to the definition of work above, almost everyone works, maybe for family and friends or as a volunteer. Some might work more, some less. Do you know someone who is not ill or handicapped who has not worked for a longer period? And before you work you have to eat, drink and sleep, so everyone needs an income. An unconditional basic income is not a social measure but would be a right of every person to be able to live with dignity. Thereafter, s/he can work as much as s/he wants or needs to. Fears evaporate, creativity arises.

In our economy almost everyone gives his potential and faculties to serve the needs of his fellow citizens all over the world. Are you aware of the fact that in every single product you find, directly or indirectly, the work of millions of people? Yes, millions of people! Would you want this to stop?

Finally our economy, which means satisfying each other's needs - not speculation with money without working yourself - has at its basis three conditions that are granted for free: natural resources, the talents of every human being, and the work of our ancestors. These should be shared in an equitable way among all human beings. So what is an UNCONDITIONAL BASIC INCOME?

"A basic income is an income unconditionally granted to all on an individual basis, without means test or work requirement. It is a form of minimum income guarantee that differs from those that now exist in various European countries in three important ways:

- *it is being paid to individuals rather than households;*
- *it is paid irrespective of any income from other sources;*
- *it is paid without requiring the performance of any work or the willingness to accept a job if offered.*

Liberty and equality, efficiency and community, common ownership of the Earth and equal sharing in the benefits of technical progress, the flexibility of the labour market and the dignity of the poor, the fight against inhumane working conditions, against the desertification of the countryside and against interregional inequalities, the viability of cooperatives and the promotion of adult education, autonomy from bosses, husbands and bureaucrats, have all been invoked in its favour.

But it is the inability to tackle unemployment with conventional means that has led in the last decade or so to the idea being taken seriously throughout Europe by a growing number of scholars and organizations. Social policy and economic policy can no longer be conceived separately, and basic income is increasingly viewed as the only viable way of reconciling two of their respective central objectives: poverty relief and full employment.

There is a wide variety of proposals. They differ according to the amounts involved, the source of funding, the nature and size of the reductions in other transfers, and in many other respects. As far as short-term proposals are concerned, the current discussion is focused on so-called 'partial basic income schemes'. These would not be full substitutes for present guaranteed income schemes but would provide a low - and slowly increasing - basis to which could be added other incomes, including the remaining social security benefits and means-tested guaranteed income supplements.

157

Many prominent European social scientists have now come out in favour of basic income - among them two Nobel laureates in economics. In a few countries some major politicians, including from parties in government, are also beginning to stick their necks out in support. At the same time, the relevant literature - on the economic, ethical, political and legal aspects - is gradually expanding and those promoting the idea, or just interested in it, in various European countries and across the world have started organizing into an active network."
(http://www.basicincome.org)

Some links:

http://en.wikipedia.org/wiki/Basic_income
http://www.youtube.com/watch?v=8jNYNMr2qaE
http://www.globalincome.org/English/BI-worldwide.html

Unconditional Basic Income in German:
"Bedingungsloses Grundeinkommen"

An interesting thought could be to pay an unconditional basic income in a regional currency (at least to some extent).

If an unconditional basic income establishes the principles of living in dignity and of being able to for others, we might need further money to realize our own project to create something new ("social innovation"). LOAN MONEY is what we need – a credit. If you have to obtain credit, interest rates are usually very high, and someone who has money to lend only gets richer. He doesn't have to work and can speculate with money at the cost of the majority of the people.

But there already exists an interesting possibility: microcredit in a regional currency.

"Regios eG" in Germany
(in german: http://www.regios.eu/mikrokredite/)
offers just such a possibility
(among others, the Chiemgauer:
http://www.chiemgauer.info/informieren/mikrokredit/).

The most interesting aspect is the absence of interest! This is done in the following way: To take into account the problem of risk, you first agree to pay interest. But at the termination of the agreement, if you fulfilled all your duties, all the interests you paid is reimbursed.

Do you agree with this statement of Rudolf Steiner?

"Steiner advocated cooperative forms of capitalism, or what might today be called stakeholder capitalism, because he thought that conventional shareholder capitalism and state socialism, though in different ways, tend to absorb the State and human rights into the economic process and transform laws into mere commodities." (Toward Social Renewal, Rudolf Steiner, Rudolf Steiner Press, 1999, page 46.)

The same Rudolf Steiner is at the origin of associative economics. *"Steiner gave a course of lectures in 1922 in which he set out his view that with the advent of global economy, the science of economics would need to take a further step, which included an elaboration of the economic process, a more precise monetary analysis, and a clearer understanding of how, through the division of labour, the associative basis of economic life becomes apparent. Associative economics emphasizes the development of conscious coordination of producers, distributors, and consumers. It understands the global economy as a single unified domain, through which human beings meet one another's needs. It is called "associative economics" because its goal is an economic sector which is managed by associations of business corporations (industry associations) and consumer associa-*

tions instead of by the Invisible Hand of the blind market (capitalist economics) and instead of by the government (socialist economics)."
(http://en.wikipedia.org/wiki/Associative_economics)

So the idea of associative economics is almost one hundred years old. The Economy for the Common Good is an idea that developed in the last few years and is nowadays critically discussed.

"An Economy for the Common Good is an alternative economic system built on values that promote the needs of the entire population. It is a tool for economic, political, and social change – a bridge to a better future.

On the economic level it is a viable and workable alternative for businesses of diverse sizes and legal structures. Its goal is to evaluate the management success of businesses based on values oriented around promoting the common good.

On the political level the movement seeks to bring about changes to current legislation. The overarching goal is to ensure a good life for all living things and for the planet as a whole, supported by a sustainable economic system. Human dignity, global fairness and solidarity, ecological sustainability, social justice, and democratic participation are at the top of the agenda.

On the social level the movement is an initiative to raise awareness for systemic change that seeks to motivate as many people as possible to cooperative, conscientious action. It is a source of hope and courage and strives to cooperate with other movements for economic, social and environmental justice.

It is an open, participative process with a grassroots structure and a global scope." ...

"While the current economic model in some cases creates prosperity, it also creates a number of serious problems: unemployment, inequality, poverty, exclusion, hunger, environmental degradation, and climate change. Social and ecological crises

161

are accompanied by three fundamental cultural crises: an existential crisis of purpose in life, a crisis of values and a crisis of democracy.

In the eyes of many observers we are dealing with a fundamental systemic crisis, which can no longer be solved by individual reforms, but only by a "system change". Besides a change in fundamental values and a change in life styles we also need an evolution in the legal framework for the economic system. According to a poll by the Bertelsmann Foundation in the summer of 2010, which was repeated in 2012, 80 to 90% of Germans and Austrians want a "new economic order".

The time is ripe for a new "great transformation" (Karl Polanyi), in the direction of embedding the economy into the social context, into the set of constitutional base values, into people's hearts and into the ecological foundations of life."

"The Economy for the Common Good is a comprehensive and coherent economic model which provides an alternative to both major historic narratives 'capitalism' and 'communism'.

• The contradictions between the goals of Western democratic constitutions and actualeconomic behaviour are addressed and resolved by a change in the legal rules for economicactivity. Incentives will be created promoting adherence to constitutional values.

• Economic success is currently measured using monetary indicators like Gross Domestic Product and financial balance sheets. Success is not measured in terms of human needs, quality of life, or the fulfilment of fundamental values but the accumulation of money. A "Common Good Product" and "Common Good Balance Sheet" would fundamentally rectify this distorted thinking and practice.

• One-sided economic thinking would be replaced by a holistic and interdisciplinary approach based on proposals founded on scientific and empirical research: game theory, neurobiology, social psychology, sociology, etc.

162

• *This is an open and evolutionary approach that promotes learning from experience and is open to integrating elements from other similar and related approaches such as the solidarity economy, economic democracy, de-growth, blue economy, care economy, gift economy, and others.*

Link: https://www.ecogood.org/

The movement, which distinguishes 20 cornerstones of this type of economy, declares that *"the Economy for the Common Good places human beings and all living entities at the centre of economic activity."* Nevertheless some critics think money still plays too big a role compared with the common good.

Campus Limpertsberg – 03 December 2013
Social Enterprise and Social Innovation
Public lecture

19.00 - 20.30, Room BS 0.04

Social business and coaching – Polygone and Inter-Actions: an integral view

As pioneers in the field of social business and social inclusion Polygone and Inter-Actions offer jobs and complementary psycho-social coaching for disadvantaged people at risk of social inclusion for over 30 years.

Experiences, challenges, chances, failures and statistics will provide an overview of experiences made in the Luxembourgish context.

The integral frame of the approach of the "Service de Consultation Socio-Pédagogique" (Inter-Actions) will be presented as well as the main difference between the philosophy of Polygone and most of the other actors in the field of social business and inclusion in the past.

Our Guest lecturers:

Dr Alfred Groff
Inter-Actions asbl, Luxembourg

Ph.D. in psychology, psychopathology and psychiatry (Paris-Lodron University in Salzburg); Special Education (The State University of New York in Albany).

Dr Alfred Groff started to work in Luxembourg in different counselling centres with the aim of integrating disadvantaged people in our society. For over 20 years he does this in the joint venture 'Inter-Actions asbl' (social work) and Polygone sàrl (economy). Having accomplished different psychotherapeutic trainings, his main interest is the integral and harmonious development of human beings (psychological, social, economical, spiritual), as he has developed in his book 'Tetranthropos, the conscious human being' (in German, 2012; in English 'Integral threefolding', a book about consciousness and self-development, democracy and money, social and solidarity economy», 2013/14)

His definition of economy is "fulfilling the needs of each other in a global network by working, meaning giving the results of our creativity and capacities to others." In this type of economy you make profits, but there is no space for financial speculation and taking from others without working for the benefit of the social network. So a healthy economy is a social economy. Social business and others social innovations hopefully facilitate a healthy economy that puts the human beings in the centre and makes a sustainable and integral development possible

Mr André Reuter
Polygone sàrl, Polysan sàrl, Mersch
Ecotec sàrl, Sanem

Degree in sociology « Sociologie urbaine et rurale » (Université Catholique de Louvain (Louvain la Neuve)) and Social Worker, Social Work, Community Development (Institut Supérieur d'Etudes Sociales de l'Etat (Bruxelles))

André Reuter and other social workers founded in 1979 the NGO Inter-Actions and from 1980 he was engaged as a social worker by Inter-Actions. His job was to organize and to empower the inhabitants of the deprived area Grund in order to improve their living conditions. He was also a member of the board of Inter-Actions

From 1995 up to today André Reuter is general manager of the different economic initiatives created by Inter-Actions: Polygone sàrl, Ecotec sàrl, Polysan sàrl

Inter-Actions

 **POLYGONE**
votre partenaire

SUSTAINABLE
DEVELOPMENT

The view of society exposed in this book was first presented at the University of Luxembourg, December 3, 2013 and the two-dimensional map of the human being at the same University, November 17, 2010 (ISBN 978-2-87971-815-6).

"Just a short note to thank you for sharing a fascinating and compelling story at the SESI session on Thursday*... it had a big impact on a lot of the students (they have integrated your story in several peer groups) and gave us all a lot to think about. Thank you for stimulating our reflections on social enterprise and CSR." (Hedda Pahlson-Moller, Business Angel / Social Investor and Impact Advisor)

*Social Enterprise and Social Innovation session on Thursday December 3, 2013

"My definition of economy is "fulfilling the needs of each other, in a global network, by working, meaning giving the results of our creativity and capacities to others." In this type of economy you make many non-financial profits, but there is no space for financial speculation and taking from others without working for the benefit of the social network. So a healthy economy is a social economy. Social enterprises and others social innovations will hopefully facilitate a healthy economy that puts the human beings in the centre and makes a sustainable and integral development possible." (Alfred M. R. Groff)

Literature for further discussion: Memenomics: The Next Generation Economic System (Said Elias Dawlabani, 2013)

6. AMOR AND RANDY

- HUMAN BEINGS IN TWO NOVELS –

6.1. Excerpts from "MENSCH, MENSCH" „AMOR and the LAST SUPPER"

**a novel about freedom, peace and love
(to be released in English)**

The people from *Tetranthropos* asked Randy and his two companions to sit with them. A woman handed out notes. The newcomers were also given a copy. "This is the paper that emerged from our preliminary meetings. We call it a DESIGN OF A FUTURE SOCIETY: The Individual and the Ideal in Society. You see three columns: the 'Freedom column' with the yellow Culture cell, the 'Equality column' with the blue State cell and the 'Solidarity column' with the red Economic cell. Today we consider the black lines of the diagram."

At the next meeting, we will talk about the third, the grey line, which deals with the role of money in society. In the session after next, we will discuss possible actions for the future, as exemplified in the fourth line."

I am self-aware === "I think" === sense of living	I relate === "I feel" === inclusion / peace	I give / I work I take / I consume === "I want" === health
We are conscious and self-determined / We are responsible **(CULTURE)**	We communicate / We decide / We control **(STATE)**	We produce / We consume / We cooperate **(ECONOMY)**
CAPITAL = AWARENESS of the entire POTENTIAL of EVERY HUMAN BEING and MUTUAL TRUST	100% MONEY / POSITIVE MONEY / FULL-RESERVE NON-SPECULATIVE BANKING === DEPRECIATING INTEREST FREE (regional) MONEY	UNCONDITIONAL BASIC INCOME for ALL to be able to work in dignity === INTEREST FREE CREDITS for COMMON WELFARE oriented ORGANISATIONS to be able to create
FREEDOM of INFORMATION === MULTI-PERSPECTIVE EDUCATION === SELF-DETERMINATION in an OPEN CULTURAL ENERGY FIELD	SIMULTANEOUS and INTEGRAL POLITICS === DIRECT / PARTICIPATORY DEMOCRACY === EVOLUTIONARY INTEGRAL ORGANISATIONS	SOCIAL and SOLIDARITY ECONOMY === ASSOCIATIVE ECONOMICS === SUSTAINABLE PRODUCING and CONSUMING
consciousness liberty creativity	democracy equal rights diversity	solidarity humanness will of life

A few month later: Randy was standing outside the white-painted front door, but before he could knock, he heard Amor's voice saying, "Come in, Randy." Amor was dressed all in white. He gave Randy a long and hearty hug.

"It's good to have you back, Randy. Have you come back from the shadowy realm?"

What did Amor mean by that? Yeah, there were many shadows in the forest.

"Shadow work is part of our efforts here, always exposing some hidden knowledge. Some time ago, I chose this place to start our project. My first partner was Peili. She supported me energetically from the beginning. First we planned the *Tetranthropos* residential community. Why *Tetranthropos*? It means: the "fourfold human being". The human is an individual, social and spiritual being, and if he manages to bring these three aspects into harmony, then he realizes and develops his sense of life. This is the path of love in its true sense, the possible fourth dimension of every human. Two hundred years ago, Goethe spoke in his "fairy tale" of love as the fourth power. Symbolically we represent this as a tetrahedron, three dimensions that meet on a higher level, whose central axis is love. We speak of "integral threefolding towards the fourth way". From "3 to 1" or very briefly "134".

Imagine the Absolute as a circle. Know what I mean?

"Well, not exactly...

"The Absolute is latent perfection. It can also be said to be the possibility of perfection from a human point of view. Man is such that he can become a worker for the Absolute. For this work, his egoism must make way for the manifestation of a higher one power that wants to happen through him. If his egoism rules, the Absolute withdraws.

Let's get back to the Absolute as a circular concept. Every living being is a point of this circle. When the being is born on this planet and has taken on a body, it is a point within the circle. When it fulfils its life purpose, the point is in the middle of the circle and is connected to its essence point in the circle of the Absolute by a straight line, the axis of love. Before this can become reality, however, man must work tirelessly on himself to become aware of himself and the work to be done. He must be prepared to take on voluntary suffering. He comes into the world with a potential, but if he neither recognizes nor develops this potential, he has not lived his possible fullness. He will go down in the history of the universe as a temporary natural phenomenon, but nothing more. The will to live always comes to him, but his own will must take on the effort to do its part in the great work.

Man is not a unity from the beginning; he has to create the unity, the harmony. The work here in *Tetranthropos* is based on a map of a human with twelve aspects. Many people see themselves and others in only one or two of the dimensions, but assume they are seeing the whole person. This is an illusion, because a partial truth can never be the truth. Which twelve aspects do I speak of? I have already mentioned the individual, the social and the spiritual levels of a human being. The individual stands, so to speak, between his spiritual and his physical nature. We like to represent the human being as three tetrahedra standing on top of each other. The top of the spiritual tetrahedron represents the transpersonal wisdom, which is divided into three parts: the will to live, diversity and creativity. The tip of the individual tetrahedron, which represents the inner life of the human being, is the Witness Ego, divided into three parts: Soul Ego, Social Ego and Body Ego. And finally, at the top of the social tetrahedron, which represents our life in society, is the human body as part of nature. With this body we are active as 'social artists' in culture, as citizens in the state and as workers in the economy. Each of these twelve aspects can again be divided into three parts. For example, the soul-ego in thinking, feeling and wanting.

But back to our community *Tetranthropos*. As you know, every house is architecturally a tetrahedron. Together we are twelve people, each one was chosen to be a partial representative of the integral human being. You live in the social house, the house of living together. I live in the spiritual house, the house of being. And Peili lives in the individual house, the house of inner becoming. In each house, the three inhabitants of the ground floor are to work together in such a way, that they do justice to the "3 to 1" and, together with the inhabitant of the upper floor, to attain the goal of the house. This means transpersonal wisdom and love in the 'Wine

House', true inner awareness for a healthy and meaningful life in the 'Water House' and harmonious and peaceful coexistence of all people in the 'Stone House'. Furthermore, colours play a certain role in our apartments. The colours of the ground floors are yellow, blue and red, each corresponding to an ideal of the French Revolution: freedom, equality and fraternity. In more contemporary terms we say: freedom, equality and humanity. But we don't want to argue about terms, it happens all too often that people mean the same thing, but fight each other most fiercely as they insist on a particular wording. Or they use woolly terms in order avoid conflict and thereby produce other problems. Back to our ideals. Since the three ideals mentioned can never be realized together, they have to be done in the right sub-area. The colours serve as a reminder. The colours of the three upper apartments - green, orange and white - have a different meaning. They stand for natural humanity, observing consciousness and true love.

By now you know who lives in which house and what colour his apartment is. But that does not matter in detail now. You just have to know that everyone within the community represents a particular aspect of a human being and he should be concerned with trying to do justice to the aim of the house. Peili and I have tried to put our community together with these considerations.

Randy, if I asked you who you were, would you answer me like most people? Like this: first they give the name of their family, then their personal name, possibly marital status. They might tell their age, how many children they have, their gender, their social status, their nationality, what worldview they have or religion they belong to and much more. What do these say? Actually only whatever roles they have taken on in their life. An enumeration of identifications, so to speak. In moments of non-identification, of silence, of introspection, they could come closer to another truth, but that makes most people too afraid. They would rather defend borders, cheer for their nation or sports club. Some are even willing to die for their interpretation of religion. They suppose this gives them security or a sense of belonging. This unconscious role identification is the cause of countless conflicts, disputes and wars. Often only words and definitions separate the different camps, and this may lead to centuries of hostility.

Randy, be yourself and live it!

Amor hugged him once more in a loving way as he said goodbye. Randy was filled with something indescribable.

ooooooo

He had worked very actively with his cohabitants in the 'stone house' on the completion of the so-called "life mandala", with extended thoughts on a future society.

The Mandala of Life

- represents the spiritual path to the CENTRE of life's endeavours. Everyday matters are unavoidable, but of secondary importance. Ultimately, the actual goal and purpose of life is the "I am", i.e. discovering, unfolding, developing and sharing one's own potentials with fellow human beings. The personality thereby enters into the service of the individual essence. That is LOVE!

- The four main areas of culture, state, economy and nature are ideally represented in the form of a TETRAHEDRON. The first three, the social areas, are lived on our planet within the framework of nature. This is to be classified on a different level, as it is the basis for social affairs. In this model, nature is located on the tip of the tetrahedron.

Similarly the inner human soul areas of thinking, feeling and wanting can be represented by the basis of a tetrahedron at the tip of which the body and its actions are located. Thinking, feeling and doing are often mentioned in the same breath. As the levels are mixed up, the will is completely forgotten.

173

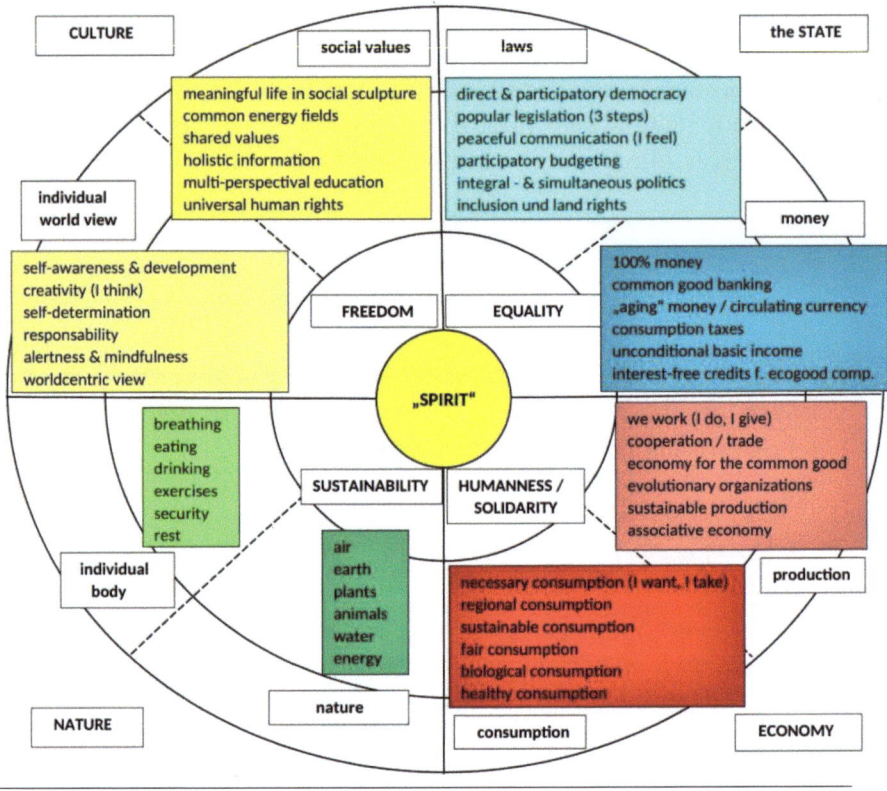

- Of course the four areas are to be seen as a WHOLE. Mostly, if not always, an event in one area cannot be seen independently of the other three. They are related.

The arrows in the mandala (see page 176) represent the relationships within one area, but of course there are also some between the areas and ideally towards the centre. The economy, for example, takes its framework from the state laws.

174

The state receives taxes from the economic sector. The products have their origin in nature, but they also need the skills from the cultural sector in the form of the skills of the people. Man, in turn, needs the economy to meet his needs. And an important question is this: Does the economy serve money or life?

In each area the others are to be found as sub-areas. For example, in a school where the cultural, the educational aspect is the main focus, there are of course also legal questions (contracts) and economic questions.

Each area must be able to conduct its affairs AUTONOMOUSLY. So: Cooperation YES, overlaps and mix-ups NO. Otherwise, the outcome will be what happened to the "mixed king" in Goethes tale of the green snake and the beautiful lily: he will collapse!

The IDEALs are different in every area. They should serve as guiding stars:

* Freedom - CULTURE ("spiritual life")

* Equal rights / Equality - STATE ("legal life")

* Humanity / Solidarity / "Brotherhood"- ECONOMY ("economic life")

* Sustainability - NATURE

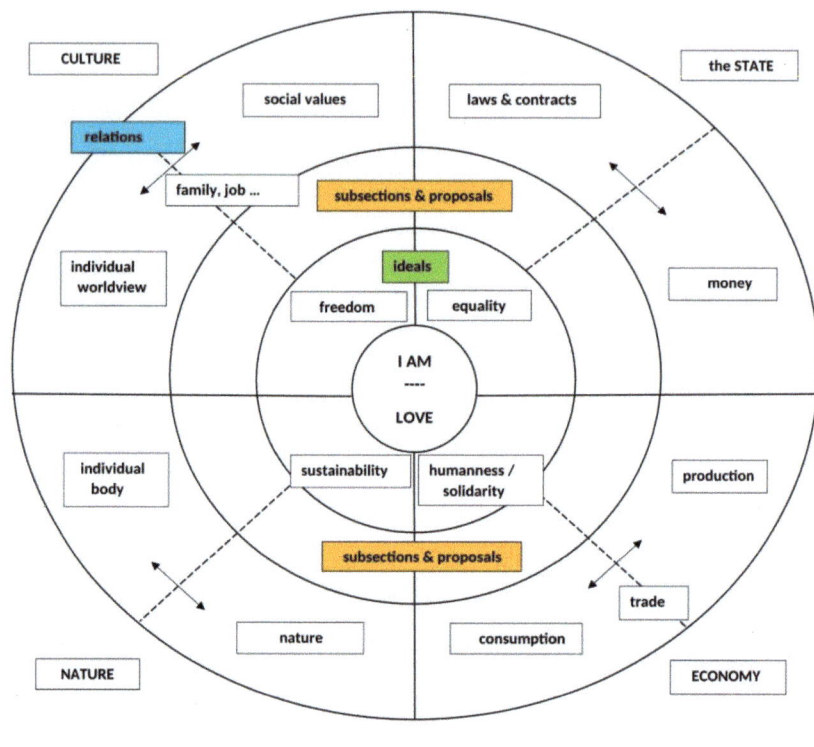

oooooooo

The day before the Last Supper, Amor went to watch the sunrise on a mountain opposite *Tetranthropos*. Once he reached the summit, he picked out a flat dry stone, sat down cross-legged and enjoyed the fresh air.

His open gaze wandered over the whole scene. From here he could see Tetranthropos below. "A view of the twelve essential perspectives of a human being, united in one community - that was my project. Whether all together could achieve the path of true love, the "3 to 1" towards the common good - that was the question. Thanks to the help of Peili, the community was launched and now it is a reality. To bring the triad into harmony, that is what we are working towards. The social, psychological and spiritual developments that everyone was striving for are well underway," he thought.

The starting signal for the integral man had been given. But Amor could neither stop nor determine the further human development. It was only clear that this would mainly have to take place outside of *Tetranthropos*. In the future everyone would leave the place and go out into the world. As an "oasis" *Tetranthropos* had no future. Man had to go into "real life", to all places, pleasant and unpleasant, beautiful and ugly, peaceful and warlike ... The experiences from *Tetranthropos* should lead to impulses for shaping the whole "social sculpture" the way Beuys, the artist understood the term "social sculpture" to embody his understanding of art's potential to transform society. Did this mean that *Tetranthropos* was doomed? Did his vision even have a future? He rummaged in his pocket and pulled out the invitation to the Last Supper. He had received that invitation a few days earlier, as had his eleven cohabitants.

At that moment, he saw a ray of sunlight reflected on the glass roof of *Tetranthropos*, and for a moment, he thought he saw a large glass tetrahedron above it. That could only be an illusion, right? The light 'spoke' to him: "The time for "4 to 1" will come soon. A future tetrahedron dedicated to research must be created in *Tetranthropos*!

In the meantime Randy rummaged in his backpack and took out an envelope that Amor had given him the day before advising him to read the contents before the Last Supper. There were three documents. First, there was a text from an online encyclopedia called 'Agape'. The second text was taken from a book by a certain Arthur Schult; an appendix entitled 'Leonardo da Vinci's Last Supper in the Light of the Starry Sky'.

Before he looked at the third one, he enjoyed a small chocolate bar. He remembered that Regina, a supporter of the idea of an unconditional basic income, had made it clear to him that millions of people are directly or indirectly involved in each product, including this chocolate. Arguments for this kind of income included both human dignity and "an income as a prerequisite for working in the global economy". To Randy's delight, such an unconditional basic income already existed in *Tetranthropos*. He even remembered that Regina had said that the economy consisted of natural resources, human abilities and ancestral work. All three were actually available to people free of charge. In her opinion, this was not sufficiently appreciated. Some profiteers and power-hungry people simply and unashamedly gain advantages at the expense of the general public.

The second document was illustrated by a picture of the twelve apostles. They were sitting together in four groups of three. The number four he discovered on the walls, the ceiling of the room, and in the folds of the tablecloth. There was something fascinating about this picture. When Randy flipped through the text and saw that there was something about zodiacs, he was immediately interested. This was also one of the new things he had experienced in the community. He knew that each of the twelve people in *Tetranthropos* had a different zodiac sign. As he read, he discovered that this was also the case with the twelve apostles in the picture.

Randy took a close look at Judas in the painting. His left hand was moving towards Jesus' right hand. Judas' right hand was holding a wallet. At least that's what he read in the accompanying text. Randy remembered that Amor had casually told him once that how an individual or a group of people handles money is a material measure of their consciousness. Money should flow for the benefit of all.

178

He dug out the third text and read the headline; 'Rose Cross, Grail and Tao'. Randy felt slightly annoyed as he leafed through the pages. He read about Percival, who went into solitude and felt the great unity of everything, experiencing himself as a centre of the forces of the all-embracing, three in particular. As he put the texts aside he wondered why Amor had given them to him. It seemed strange to compare the signs of the zodiac of the apostles with those of the inhabitants of *Tetranthropos*. Randy suddenly felt drowsy while reading and fell asleep. He dreamed of sitting at the Last Supper with his eleven cohabitants in *Tetranthropos*, just like in Leonardo's picture with the Apostles. Jesus' chair was empty …

And so it happened…

6.2. EXCERPTS FROM „ICH BIN. MENSCH"

"RANDY and the STREAM OF LIFE"

a novel about birth, death, time and future
(to be released in English)

Kena continued, "I dreamt last night that Amor was talking to me. and..."

"Gross! What did he say? ..." Nexus interrupted her impatiently.

"I'd like to tell you if you'd let me finish. Amor said something like this: A circle can shrink to a point, and the point can expand to a circle. This is an image for the pulsation between the self and the universe. In the space between the circle and its centre point, one can imagine the ups and downs of everyday life, as well as - like a big hurdle - the shadow parts of our personality that hinder access to our essence. Through the third dimension, there is the possibility to raise the circle to the spiral, the spiral of development towards the axis of love, which has as its final goal the Higher I. Why am I telling all this?

You want to build a new house. A house where the next generation, the generation of the future, will grow up. Imagine that the base of the planned tetrahedron starts to rotate. This creates a circle around the three corners of the tetrahedron. Imagine a spiral vortex upwards, which is created along the edges of the tetrahedron. The tetrahedron thus turns into a cone. You can understand its axis as the representation of evolution and involution, but also of life or love. The tetrahedron is angular, male and a cone is round and female.

The new house must have the shape of a cone that encompasses a tetrahedron. In this way your further development and dynamics can become visible in the architecture! The form becomes more complex, like your individual and social development. You could call it a "human courtyard house."

oooooo

Amor: "Nice to see you Peili, it's been a while. I would like to give you some messages that will be important for you in the future. I

182

will keep it short, just listen. At the Last Supper you received the message that Rosalba would take my place among you. This will take quite some time, but it will not be as you probably imagine. She will not live and work in the Institute in Tetranthropos to explore the twelve basic aspects of being in her visible manifestations. Nor will she go out to bring these into the world and network. *You* will do that. I hereby appoint you the first Minister of Foreign Affairs of Tetranthropos. Rosalba will try to observe and develop the 12 aspects within herself in the extended community. For this she will need all her strength. But as my Interior Minister she will manage it with my help.

Meanwhile, Randy was sitting comfortably at the foot of one of the pyramids. He could never have dreamed that he would travel to such a place. As he let his gaze wander over the breath-taking surroundings, an attractive woman came and sat down next to him. She seemed to be Egyptian, but addressed Randy in English. How did she know Randy's language?

"Hello, I am Hathor. Do you like our pyramids?"

"Hi, I'm Randy... uh... sure. Looks like you do, too."

"Yes, and there's a reason for that. I've been studying the writings of the Russian author Ouspensky. You wouldn't know him, would you?"

"Never heard of him."

"Recently I studied his theory that in remote times religion, philosophy, art and science were one and the same as a way to the truth. Now the four areas not only differ from each other more and more, but are split up into many subgroups. This will make it more and more difficult to find the truth."

"Aah... and what does this have to do with the pyramids?" Randy couldn't figure out what this Hathor woman wanted from him.

"Look, the pyramids have four edges, and they meet at the top. Two edges can represent intellectual access to truth, philosophy and science. The other two are for emotional access, religion and art."

"I think the pyramids are great, but I like the tetrahedrons better."

Randy was amazed when she said, "I know. You can also think of the top of the tetrahedron as a place of "truth". The edge that stands for religion and philosophy, then corresponds to the spiritual approach. Both are concerned with spiritual ideas, the one being the revelations of higher messengers and the other being input, which thoughtful people receive as a gift, so to speak. The edges for art and science correspond to the mental and material access to truth."

"Why are you telling me all this?" Randy asked.

"Because I love you, that's what I do best."

With this Hathor gave Randy a kiss on the forehead and disappeared into the mass of tourists.

ooooooo

Sometime later Georg invited a small circle of interested people to his house. The topic of the day was: 'Ts Triple Tetrahedron Tone, the Triad'. T would introduce the evening with the lecture: 'How Sounds and Planets Shape Developmental Processes'.

Georg briefly introduced T and concluded by saying, "T will be happy to answer questions afterwards. T, you have the floor."

"I would now like to talk about my vision of the Triple Tetrahedron Tone process. Some people call me T just because of this. Let me start with a little warning: Do not expect to understand everything right away. To fully understand the laws of world creation and preservation, as well as the personal evolution of man, is a lifelong task.

Well then, here we go:

There are three points at the base of a tetrahedron and the fourth point is at the top of this three-sided pyramid. The axis in the middle goes through this raised point. I call it the axis of love. This is where the triad becomes harmony."

184

George wondered if T was in contact with Amor. He had so often said similar things.

"For a long time, I have tried in vain to draw a tetrahedron with only one stroke, so that I never had to put the pencil down. I succeeded only when I included love. This laid the foundation for depicting the physical, mental and spiritual development of the human being as a threefold process. Sounds can play just as interesting a role in the visual representation as the planets".

T stepped up to the blackboard that Georg had provided. He would supplement his explanations with some drawings.

"At the beginning of a man's transformation into his true self, there is the sound DO. It represents 'Being'. Only when the other tones develop from the DO, does evolution take place. From the Do we draw a line diagonally downwards: the tone RE arises. The impulse of Mars, the action planet, is at work. It shoots an arrow out of the DO.

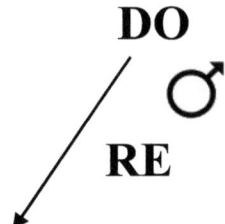

Then, we draw an equally long line diagonally upwards, which represents the tone MI. The impulse from Mars is interrupted by Saturn. This planet stands for boundaries and restrictions, also for structures.

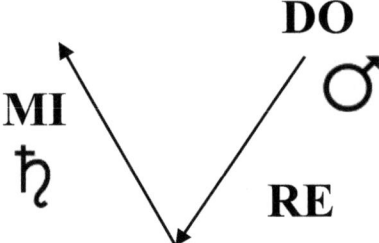

Without structure, every action, just like freedom, would be lost in a thousand possibilities. In everyday life people take action, but certain difficulties or obstacles arise in the implementation of the project. Some then just give up on what they have started. This is their reactive, mostly unconscious personality at work.

Between MI and FA a semitone is missing in the DUR scale. Now it needs an impulse from outside. Otherwise there is the threat of a standstill. In myths, at this moment, a light, a fairy, or a wise man appears. Imagine the two lines already drawn as two of three lateral edges of a tetrahedron whose tip points to the bottom. Then Mercury and Venus, hand in hand, join to help. Mercury, the planet of mediation, leads to the centre of the base of the tetrahedron, where the axis of love is located. This centre is the fifth point in the tetrahedron, the five being a symbol for man.

Now imagine Venus, the planet of love. Its energy strives through the 'love axis', which unites the trinity in unity, down to the top of the tetrahedron.

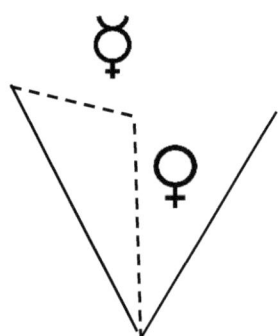

Here the tone FA sounds. Love enables FA to step through the gate to a new dimension. Jupiter appears. This enhances the process by making it possible to create a three-dimensional shape from the tip by adding the third edge of the tetrahedron. The triangle raised in this figure is the base of the tetrahedron, which contains the tones SOL, LA and SI on its legs.

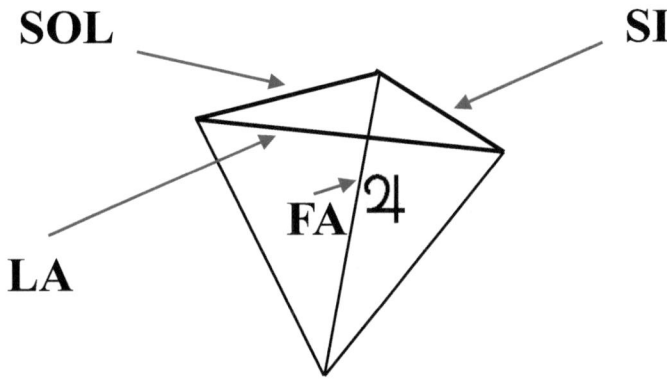

Thus we have arrived at the level of light, where the moon and the sun dance. SOL representing the sun, moves on the first leg of the triangle. From the perspective of 'Spiral Dynamics', a theory about the development of levels of worldview, only from here on an 'evolutionary-integral view of second order' is possible. I am no longer biased in my 'first order' subjective view and believe that it is the best or only correct one. But I do not want to go into this theory now. What is important is that on this level all views appear in a new light. There is a radical change in the level of consciousness. Linear thinking is transformed into multidimensional thinking.

The process is not yet complete, because the moon still has to be integrated.

The moon represents the personality part that has not yet placed itself in service to essence, the sunlike core of a human being.

Remember the image on my T-shirt of the two hands pointing to each other from Michelangelo's fresco 'The creation of Adam'".

He pulled the shirt from his pocket and held it up.

The hand of Adam represents the essential motivation of the human being, the will that drives the development of the process, represented by the sound LA. This runs along the second leg of the triangle, the motivation fueled by the goal of fulfilling one's life purpose.

SI, along the third limb of the triangle, strives towards the tone DO and since another semitone is missing between the two tones, help is needed again, this time starting from the DO, which, so to speak, extends the second hand. Here it is crucial to open up inwardly, not to be too absorbed in self-referential actions, so that one can also perceive the hand stretched out in the opposite direction. If you do this, you know that you are on the right path. This helps to cover the last stretch of this first cycle. SI leads you to the first sub-goal. The index fingers of the two hands touch each other.

This evolved tone DO is located one triangle apex further than the original DO. But the journey is not over. Two more passages through the tetrahedron are still to come. The 'process of the three DOS', the process of 'evolving in being' from the physical to the mental to the spiritual level, leads back to the original DO. We already called this: 'from three to one'. The outstretched hand contains the impulse to push another octave cycle. However, the person must be willing to work consciously and to suffer. He is not spared this. But once he has completed another cycle, the third cycle is just around the corner. One can always imagine that one has already reached the goal in order to energize the process, but one has to remember that one is still on the way. After passing through the third octave, the triangle apex of the original DO is reached. The human being has arrived. Only now can he say: 'I am'.

DO1 could be called a solar eclipse. Agnes Hydveghy, who has inspired my life companion, speaks of the 'sun behind the sun' which is not revealed to our consciousness. DO2 could be called the

188

crescent moon, which partially reflects the sun, and DO3 the full moon, which completely reflects the sun. DO4, the original DO, is the true Sun, which has become fully conscious of itself.

These are certainly not simple images I am presenting to you. They symbolize our potentials. The third octave will probably remain unattainable for the vast majority of people.

And you know that such 'maps' cannot replace reality and your own experience. However, they do make it possible to orientate yourself. The danger is that you break up reality into parts and perceive only the interesting aspects. But life can only be understood as a whole and not from its parts or models".

I would like to conclude our excursion into possible areas of human development with a map which I call 'The development of the true human being' ..."

	„I am" – Part of the Absolute (Core of my essence)	
„the spiritual body"		*„third octave"*

TRIAD: spirit man / life spirit / spirit self - Kether / Chochmah / Binah -

	Awareness/ Witness / neutral OBSERVER	
„the soul body"		*„second octave"*

CONSCIOUSNESS: objective integral knowledge ⇧	INDIVIDUALITY: objective feeling ⇧	WILL: direction/ aim of the core of my essence ⇧
subjective comparisons/ judgments/ opinions	subjective sympathies/ antipathies (subpersonalities)	pers. wishes/lusts/ instinctive impulses
body-knowledge (comportment studies)	body-feeling (inner sensing)	adequate use of the body (experimentation)
system of nerves and senses (perceptions/thoughts)	breathing and circulation system (life force/flow of energy)	system of metabolism and limbs

„the physical body"	body – part of nature & the material world: the DEEDs	*„first octave"*
		„ideals"

freedom in the culture i.a. education matters (potentials/creativity)	equality in money- and legislation matters (relationships/communication)	solidarity/common good in the economy (needs)
senselessness instead of free pursuit of my aims	solitude instead of inclusion in peace	illness/death instead of health

„fears"

190

○○○○○○○

Regina, whose favourite theme has always been 'Democracy and Money', and Kushala have drawn up the 'Free and Equal Manifesto' or the 'Manifesto for Cultural Freedom, for Equality in a Participatory Democracy and for Solidarity in an Economy of Common Good'. Kushala was in charge of the cultural questions as prerequisites for the topic 'Democracy and Money'. Reginas and Kushalas favourite questions to their fellow human beings are

CULTURAL QUESTIONS
(Requirements for the topic "democracy and money")

Do we want ...

1. Free schools (not to be confused with private schools) and free research.
2. Education vouchers for all citizens and for all levels of education Right to train their skills and preferences.
3. Lifelong integral education (multi-perspectival / world-centric view) and training.
4. Free access to information (free Internet access for all / no intellectual property / freedom of the press / libraries and cultural activities for all ...) and a transparent flow of information.
5. Use the term 'work' correctly
(labour is not a commodity / negotiated profit sharing instead of wage labour) and use the term 'money' correctly (money is not a commodity / money is a circulating legal document regulating the flow of goods and services).
6. Individual human rights with an unconditional basic income as a basic right for a free individual development and a humane existence without fear for survival.

7. The inclusion of all people, since every person is an artist (has skills / creativity ...)?

and questions about DEMOCRACY and MONEY

Do we want ...

1. A right of initiative and a three-step citizens' legislation (with adequate quorums, long exchange phases, balanced information on factual issues and binding decision).

2. Participatory budgeting, in which, in addition to financial, social and ecological aspects must be taken into account.

3. Citizen forums and participation in all relevant future issues, e.g. land ownership reform, as well as the creation of framework conditions that promote the social commitment of citizens.

4. A 'simultaneous policy' (Simpol) against destructive global competition and for cooperation in worldwide environmental and financial issues, in poverty reduction.

5. '100% money' and exclusive money creation (coins, notes and book money) by the central banks, which fully secures all savings in the event of a private bank bankruptcy.

6. Neutral, flowing, ageing money, e.g. regional currencies with circulation hedging instead of exponential compound interest.

7. Transparency of all cash flows to a certain extent and an end to tax havens.

8. Different independent types of banks according to their function, e.g. separation of banks with a link to the real economy from those with activities in the speculative economy.

9. Interest-free loans and donations (in the form of state tax benefits or tax-privileged donations) for solidarity-based, sustainably working and charitable projects and companies, which belong neither to private individuals nor to the state, but to the general public or in other words their own *raison d'être*.

10. Consumption taxes instead of wage taxes, with zero taxation on essential goods, with environmental protection taxes, with a high taxation on luxury goods, as well as a maximum taxation on speculative banking transactions.

11. Freedom of tax choice, i.e. the choice of which areas of society (state budgets) the taxes to be paid go to.

12. Setting an individual maximum income and capital accumulation limit?

ooooooo

Ten years later:

From these conversations, Kevin's ten psychological messages developed over time. He enthusiastically presented them to everyone and passionately discussed them.

1. Do what you really want, that is your life-task - be a true individual - think, feel and follow the will of your conscience before you act.

2. Live in reality in the here and now without illusions, act against the negative and enjoy the positive.

3. Act only consciously and fall as little as possible into identifications and projections.

4. Trust yourself and the universe, be connected with it in love, everything additional is a gift.

5. Observe yourself on all levels as often as you can - physically, mentally, spiritually and socially.

6. Avoid negative emotions like anger, lamentation, jealousy, envy ..., be positive and smile at the world, its challenges are given chances.

7. Omit justifying explanations, just do it better next time, get to know your dark sides.

8. Consider all possible perspectives before you act, this way you will become free and see all your possibilities.

9. Create free space inside yourself and listen with open ears, so you will know what the future wants from you.

10. Don't forget that your evaluations shape your reality and often waste your energy, because reality is what it is and you often cannot change it; what you see in the other person is probably yourself.

7. SOME FINAL THOUGHTS

**REMEMBER, "I AM" TETRANTHROPOS
THE CONSCIOUS HUMAN BEING!**

**If you don´t WORK on it every hour for the rest of your life,
it won't WORK.**

Stop identifying with all and everything.

ACT being "IN LOVE"

"I DO WHAT I AM"

LISTEN to the call from the FUTURE!

Integral

"I" consciously develop
"higher, wider and deeper" realities.
"I", the *integral* ray of LOVE, the ONE.
There is no 2, no duality.
Two can't be without relationship in a common 'field',
so there are always 3.

3 folding

I co-create the "free, equal and human" field we live in.
The essence of *threefolding* is the way of LOVE.

4th way

I am, can (think), feel, want, do, serve on the axis of love.
I bow to LIFE!

INTEGRAL is defined here as seeing a whole from as many perspectives as possible, with a consciousness of maximal depth and width, and from a cosmo-centric point of view.

To understand a whole it helps to differentiate its main aspects. If we differentiate THREE aspects, we can speak of THREEFOLD-ING. If ONE represents the ABSOLUTE, THREE represents the triad that stands for the three main forces in the universe.

In this book we played. We symbolically combined the THREE vertices of a triangle at its centre and we came to point number FOUR. The elevated middle of the triangle led us to a TETRAHEDRON, the axis of which we defined as an emanation of the ONE and that we called the "axis of LOVE". We move towards the FOURTH WAY!

In his lecture in Wangen ("nine eleven" - "1984") entitled *"Die Frage nach dem Sinn der Technik"* the German artist Johannes Stüttgen reflected on Andy Warhol's saying „*I would like to be a machine*". If you say this, it means you are a human being! Normally people would say "*I don't like to be a machine*". Are they afraid of becoming one? A machine is selfless and serves.

What do we need today? Serving one another as an act of real love? Find the vision that is consistent with your transpersonal core and make it happen!

… Being is always working in us, trying to break through the hard crust of our ego into the light of consciousness. The primordial impetus animating human will is the striving of being toward the light. Thus it is not our efforts that produce the experience of being. They simply prepare the way. The experience is not of our doing, but a revelation of <u>what is</u>. If we repeat unceasingly our efforts — and they need to be repeated — it is to learn to let the reality of Being emerge.
We wish to try to open without fear, to open not once or twice but constantly, until we become conscious of the power of the ego which separates us from life. We undertake this adventure of opening in order to know all the signs by which Being makes itself felt. We learn not to look at ourselves as the measure of all things and as the master of our lives. We begin to feel that we can participate in a great unity, a great Whole."

(Jeanne de Salzmann, The reality of being, p.280f.)

Alfred M.R. GROFF , Ph.D.

www.alfredgroff.com

Ph.D. in psychology, psychopathology and psychiatry
(Paris-Lodron University Salzburg /
State University of New at Albany)

Psychotherapist
(http://www.collegemedical.lu / 2016.12.016 / PSYCHO)

Author of different books
(topics: the human being - democracy - unconditional basic income)

Main interest: the integral and harmonious development of human
beings (psycho-spiritual and socio-economical) and the inclusion of
all in our societies